# Come Out[illegible]



## Is[illegible] Chapman

PO Box 10
Ulverston
Cumbria
LA12 8HR
England

Trade distribution through:
New Wine Ministries
PO Box 17,
Chichester
PO20 6RY
England



Bible quotations are from the Authorised Version.

ISBN 0 947852 44 1

Typeset by CRB Typesetting Services, Ely, Cambridgeshire

# Contents


| Chapter | | Page |
|---|---|---|
| | Introduction | 1 |
| 1. | Come out of Her, My People | 5 |
| 2. | More than the Mother of Jesus | 19 |
| 3. | Justification by Faith | 25 |
| 4. | Purgatory versus Heaven or Hell | 31 |
| 5. | In Remembrance and Memorial of Him | 53 |
| 6. | The Great Apostasy | 77 |
| 7. | The Spirit of Truth | 137 |
| 8. | The Woman of the Apocalypse | 161 |
| | Books and videos available | 181 |

# Acknowledgements

I wish to express my deep gratitude and thanks to Ron Taylor. For eight years we have laboured together in the Lord's service, and during the passing of those years, I can honestly say that I have never once heard him complain.

Regardless of trials and opposition he has stood firm on Christ, his Rock, and fought the good fight of faith. Throughout the years he has been a constant source of help and encouragement in so many different ways. Keep it up Ron, I still need you! – Remember Moses was 120 etc! – you still have a long way to go!

There is a worldly expression that goes something like this: 'Behind every good man there is a good woman,' and this is certainly the case in Ron's situation. Thank you Jean for your love, your patience, your goodness and being the 'good woman' in Ron's life.

I also wish to express my deep gratitude and thanks to Daphne, my helper and companion in the Lord's service. I continue to thank God for the day He brought us together.

Despite trials and opposition she has faithfully stood firm, wanting only to walk in obedience and fulfil God's call in her life. Without counting cost to self she has daily encouraged me to 'go on' and 'contend for the faith, which was once delivered unto the saints.'

Her patient endurance and help in presenting this book has been varied and most valuable. Thank you Daphne!

A very special 'thank you' to Jan Owbridge, who in the midst of her own busy schedule in the Lord's service, very efficiently converted my hand-written manuscript into typescript.

Over the years Jan has proved to be a trusty and reliable co-worker in Christ. Bless you and thank you, Jan.

Sincere and grateful thanks to my Mother and faithful team of intercessors. I thank God upon every remembrance of you all!

Last, but not least, I wish to thank Ed. Harding and Jan Rees for their most valuable help and words of wisdom.

# Introduction

Books which point out error are often perceived as unhelpful and divisive, yet the Scriptures clearly show that the Body of Christ needs to hold uncompromisingly to the Word of Life. All Scripture is God-breathed and useful for teaching, rebuking, correcting and training in righteousness (2 Tim 3:16).

It is against that standard that we have to test ALL things, and none of us is immune, even in the interests of unity. Paul writes that regrettably there has to be division, or separation, to show who will hold to the Word of God and who will not.

We live in days when ecumenism and unity (syncretism) have taken priority over biblical truth, and where compromise and negotiation have sought to bring about a superficial and unbiblical unity. Truths which saints of the past laid down their lives for in martyrdom are now traded as negotiable to establish an outward unity to the world.

The true unity of the believers is One Lord, One Faith, One Baptism and the unity of the Spirit among born-again believers is automatic (Ephesians 4), when we have the same Lord and are born from above by the same incorruptible seed, for we have the same Father. Claiming to believe in God or even that Jesus is the Son of God is not enough. The

Devil believes these things too, so the question for the basis of fellowship and unity is 'Have you been born again through repentance and faith?' If not you are not a genuine part of the Body of Christ.

Parallel to the Bride of Christ we are told that the one world Apostate Church will be formed by the Spirit of Antichrist. Antichrist means OTHER Christ, not AGAINST Christ as often supposed, and it will be a system not built on the Jesus of the Scriptures but, nevertheless, using his name among unregenerate participants. It will be a religious counterfeit, and to those in it Jesus will say, 'You are of your father, the Devil. Depart from me. I never knew you.'

The current spirit of the age makes it hard for us to accept that God would do this, but the warnings in Scripture are there to alert us.

Both the Scriptures (Revelation 17) and history indicate the Apostate Church to be the Church of Rome, she who sits on seven hills (Rev 17:9), clothed in scarlet (Rev 17:4), dripping with the blood of martyrs (Rev 17:6).

The reformers never accepted Rome as a Christian denomination, as is currently happening, in the belief that there has been a fundamental change in attitude and doctrine.

The purpose of this book is to alert believers to what is happening, and to show from the Scriptures that no such change has in fact occurred. The current strategy of Rome is to draw evangelical believers into her arms by blurring the differences between Roman doctrine and biblical truth. The strategy has radically changed from persecution to one of warmth and welcome; and because evangelicals of course want unity, and to contribute to a united church to present to the world after so many years of division, they respond equally warmly.

Those who stand for purity and holiness in the Bride of Christ are swimming against the tide and constantly criticized as divisive.

My concern is to warn those who remain within the doctrine of Rome of the words of Jesus,

*'Come out of her, my people! lest you be defiled'*.

Let not your pure streams of the river of life be polluted or defiled. One stream cannot produce both fresh and brackish water. Where they mix both end up impure. I call you to draw from the well of salvation, to be obedient to the Holy Spirit, to the Lord, and to His eternal Word. If you have ears to hear, hear what the Spirit is saying to the Bride.

# *Chapter One*

# Come out of Her, My people

Did it really happen or was it just a bad dream? When not wanting to face up to the consequences of a horrific situation, it is easy to blot it out from one's memory and hide it in the deep recesses of the soul.

I did not want to remember the abominations that we had witnessed on that Good Friday in Manila, which I knew to be a stench in the nostrils of God.

The events of that day were so evil and totally instigated by Satan, the enemy of the Gospel of Jesus Christ, I determined never again to think about it, far less speak about it.

Yet I came to realise that the Lord had not led me to witness that diabolical scheme without a purpose, and He reminded me:

> *'My thoughts are not your thoughts, neither are your ways my ways, for as the heavens are higher than the earth, so are my ways higher than your ways, and my thoughts than your thoughts.'* (Isaiah 55:8–9)

For eight months after my return from the Philippines, the events of that day remained a carefully guarded secret which, through the passing of time, had sunk into oblivion.

> *'a man's heart deviseth his way, but the Lord directs his steps.'* (Prov 16:9)

Under the direction of the Lord, I set aside time to edit the yards of film taken by Philip White during our second mission to the Philippines. There on the screen, the reality of the diabolical events of that day in Manila were once again revealed. The recollections of that day flooded my mind.

We had arranged to meet Pastor Isaguirre at 9.30 am on the morning of that day – the day I had tried to blot out from my memory.

'Sister Chapman', he said, 'I feel led of the Lord to drive you and your team to the other side of town. You need to witness for yourselves the evil that is practised here, under the banner of the Church of Rome. A large number of the Catholic population do not fully agree with all the religious rites which you will see practised, yet the leaders of the Church have done nothing to try to put a stop to it for it is a longstanding tradition that takes place every Good Friday in many different places throughout the islands of the Philippines.'

The appointed meeting place was a Roman Catholic Church on the outskirts of Manila. Even though we had arrived early, hundreds of people had already gathered there.

There were those who had come with the intention of using the day to gain a few extra pesos. Some had drinks for sale, others ice cream, green mangoes or nuts; anything they thought would sustain the onlookers as they stood through the scorching heat of the day.

The people seemed to be in a great state of excitement as they waited for the events of the day to commence. There was a definite carnival atmosphere in the air, and men with trays of trinkets for sale pushed their way through the jostling, noisy crowd as children unconcernedly sailed pieces of stick and paper in the puddles of polluted water that were everywhere.

Suddenly, our attention was drawn to the Church: a group of singers within attempted to harmonize chants into microphones which were relayed out to the crowds. From time to time they changed shifts and as we made our way up the steps into the church they began to sing 'Ave Maria'.

There in front of us stood an altar approximately fifteen feet long, adorned with many idols. There were beautiful idols of a woman and child, which obviously represented the Virgin Mary and Jesus. There were idols of men representative of many saints; there were idols of a baby king dressed up in kingly robes, with a crown on its head. There was a huge idol of a man, dragging a cross, with blood dripping from his knees.

The noise of the 'out of tune' singers, the sight of all these idols and the strong feeling of oppression that threatened to engulf us quickly drove us from the church.

As we dismounted the steps our attention was drawn to a man-sized idol which was being paraded through the street on a trailer. The idol was of a bearded man, neatly dressed in a blue skirt and gold wrap around its shoulders.

The oppression was becoming almost tangible. I did not want to be involved with or even to look upon another of these idols, which I knew were contemptible in the sight of God. Flicking through the pages of my Bible, seeking a word from the Lord, I started to read Jeremiah 10:2–5:

> *'Thus saith the Lord, "Learn not the way of the heathen and be not dismayed at the signs of heaven; for the heathen are dismayed at them. For the customs of the people are vain: for one cutteth a tree out of the forest, the work of the hands of the workman, with the axe.*
>
> *They deck it with silver and with gold; they fasten it with nails and with hammers, that it move not.*
>
> *They are as upright as the palm tree, but speak not; they must needs be borne, because they cannot go. Be not afraid of them, for they cannot do evil, neither also is it in them to do good.*
>
> v11.
>
> *Thus shall ye say unto them, The gods that have not made the heavens and the earth, even they shall perish from the earth and under these heavens." '*

The shrill sound of a loudly blown whistle broke my concentration. The sound had caught everyone's attention and caused the hundreds of bystanders to raise their voices in great excitement. This was obviously that for which they had been waiting. The crowd flocked towards the area that had been roped off.

The sight that met my eyes as I looked along the street left me speechless, and I stared in shocked amazement. Daphne turned to me and said,

'This can't really be happening. I'm sure we'll wake up and find it is just a bad dream'.

It wasn't a dream. Four young men were crawling slowly and painfully along the street on their knees in the direction of the church. As they crept closer we could see that they were carrying whips, made of ten leather thongs, with which they whipped their bare backs.

The crowds pressed forward, straining against the officials trying to keep them back into some kind of line. Children were forgotten as their elders elbowed their way forward trying to get a better view of the action, anxious to ensure that the young men were really punishing themselves.

Having overcome the initial shock of this barbaric sight, I turned to the man standing next to me,

'Why are they doing this?' I asked.

He just happened to be able to understand and speak the English language.

'As a penance for their sins', he proudly stated.

'Penances cannot wipe out their sins', I told him, 'Jesus shed His sinless blood to wipe out our sins. Only His blood was an acceptable offering. He shed His blood once, for all. Penances deny the sufficiency of the sacrifice of Jesus!'

He answered, 'Yes, some people believe that, but we believe in the sacrament of penance; it is taught by our Church.'

By this time the four deluded young men had reached the roped off area in front of the church. There they were received by both men and women carrying whips, before whom they prostrated themselves, and each one was lashed twelve times across the buttocks; and as they lay there, flat on their faces, we saw the ugly weal marks drip with blood, caused by the self-inflicted flagellations.

Other officials closely examined their backs, wiping off the blood in order to make sure that the weals were still oozing with fresh blood.

Daphne, Sheila and I felt physically sick. Phil turned grey. We had seen more than enough to convince us that these penances were totally evil and barbaric.

The man standing next to me began to give me a running commentary of the events. Pointing to the victims lying face down on the ground he said:

'These men have committed many bad sins. Through the sacrament of penance they will be forgiven.'

He was trying to convince me that I was wrong and he was right. At that moment the deluded men rose to their knees and crawled into the church. Once again they lay flat on their faces, and each was lashed another twelve times.

The commentary from my neighbour continued:

'Now they are being lashed for the sick members of their families; we believe that this penance will save the fate of their families and bring them health and good luck'.

It was obvious that he completely believed what he was explaining to me. I was appalled by such deception, and explained to him that what he believed was in total opposition to the scriptural truth of the gospel of grace.

The prostrating ceremony was now over. The four deluded young men were once again on their knees. They crawled up to the altar, flogging their backs with their whips. Upon reaching the altar they rose to their feet, bowed before the Host and kissed the feet of the many idols.

The ordeal for them was now over . . . until the next Good Friday. As they walked out of the church they removed the black veils which had covered their faces. Now they could show their faces in public, believing that they had been vindicated by their penances.

In spite of the fact that they must have been aching all over because of their self inflicted wounds and twenty four lashes, their faces broke into great smiles, their eyes shone with looks of victorious selfrighteousness.

The worst was yet to come. Throughout the whole day at fifteen minute intervals, groups of self flagellators arrived at the church, where the satanic penance ritual was repeated. The choir wailed on in their shifts, trying to maintain a religious atmosphere.

At approximately 2 pm, the scene was being set for the main attraction of the day. Three men appeared carrying a large wooden cross. The cross was wiped clean of the dust and blood stains of the previous year's victim, with a dirty rag. The crowd worked themselves into a state of emotional excitement. They pushed, shoved, shouted and fought with each other for the position that would offer the best view of the atrocity that was about to take place.

Men dressed as Roman soldiers were leading a young man towards the cross. The victim lay down on the cross, positioning his feet on the purpose-built pedestal which had been firmly fixed to the vertical beam of the cross.

The pedestal would ensure that the weight of his body would not hang on the nails. After his feet were carefully positioned, he was secured by a rope round the ankles. He stretched out his arms and they were securely tied to the cross.

Another man appeared, wielding a hammer in one hand and two six inch nails in the other. It was obvious that the victim was heavily drugged; his eyes rolled in his head. The older man with the hammer and nails was to assist the victim to fulfil the sacrament of penance by nailing the victim to the cross.

The older man very carefully positioned the six inch nail on the centre of the outstretched palm. One, two, three sharp blows with the hammer and the young man's left hand was nailed to the cross. The same procedure was carried out on the right hand. The victim never uttered a sound.

The cross with the young man nailed to it was hoisted into the upright position by a rope secured to the roof of the church. He hung there through the long, hot afternoon, vainly believing, in his ignorance of the truth, that he was pleasing God.

We were disgusted and sickened and could not understand how a *Christian* denomination, namely the Roman Catholic church, allowed such atrocities in this day and age.

I cried out to the Lord, 'Why? why? why does the Pope not put an end to these evil penances?'

I remembered during my first visit to the Philippines how the Pope's visit had taken precedence over every other situation. The people flocked from all over the islands to get a glimpse of the one they called *Our Most Holy Father*. I had heard no report of rebuke or condemnation by the Pope against these abominations that take place regularly every Good Friday in the Philippines.

It was not easy to get away from the horrific scene we had just witnessed. We literally had to push our way through the crowds, to the place where we had left the jeepney.

Once inside the jeepney I asked Pastor Isaguirre, 'Will they leave the young man on the cross until he dies?'

'No, they will leave him there for two or three hours, and an ambulance will be waiting to take him to hospital', he replied. 'Approximately eighteen other victims would have been nailed to crosses in different areas throughout our islands today,' he explained.

Since then I have found out that the same satanic religious rites are practised in Spain and South America.

We were weaving our way in the jeepney, at walking pace, through the crowds. As we entered the main highway we were engulfed in a tidal wave of humanity. It was incredible. As far as the eye could see, people filled the six lane highway in a solid block. Pastor Isaguirre very carefully negotiated the jeep through hundreds of thousands of people. The biggest majority of this tidal wave of humanity were carrying large wooden crucifixes or statues of Mary.

‘Where are these people going?’ I asked the Bible students who accompanied us.

‘They are on a walk of penance which will end with an open air mass on top of that hill you see in the distance.’

The Bible students started to shout Bible texts to the crowd as we weaved our way through them. Daphne was concerned that their cries of ‘God hates idolatry’, ‘You must be born again,’ and ‘Jesus is the only way’ might make the crowd angry.

‘They could so easily overturn the jeep and trample us into the ground’, she said.

The crowd’s reaction was quite different from what she expected. They looked at us with disdain, lost in the self-righteousness of their walk of penance. After all, we were the only people going in the opposite direction.

Pastor Isaguirre, concerned that the jeep might overheat, tried to speed up by taking to the side streets, but they were equally congested. The following day newspapers reported that over a million people had taken to the streets the previous day.

## The Sacrament of Penance

Through viewing the film, the memories of that dreadful day had once again been brought to the forefront of my mind. So many questions filled my heart. Why had the Lord led Pastor Isaguirre to drive us to the other side of town to witness these evil penances? Why did the Lord ensure that the scene was captured on film? The film would bring no glory to the Lord Jesus; all it could be used for would be to expose the works of darkness. I racked my brains trying to think of how such a film could be used in Britain. Could it be used within the Roman Catholic Church here, to draw attention to what was happening in the Philippines and put an end to the satanic sacrament of penance?

It seemed preposterous to even think that the Body of Christ in Britain would be involved in this sacrament, which denied the sufficiency of the sacrifice of Jesus Christ. I felt sure that the beliefs of Catholic brethren in Britain bore no resemblance to the beliefs of Filipino Catholics. There was only one answer: to pray and wait on the Lord's guidance. In the meantime, I decided to put the film on one side.

Some days later the postman delivered a package addressed to me. The postmark revealed that it had been sent from the Channel Islands. Opening the wrappings I found a book inside, the title of which was, 'Fifty Years in the Church of Rome' by Charles Chiniquy. It was a thick book and, turning to the last page, I saw that there were three hundred and sixty pages. When would I ever find time to read such a long book in the midst of a busy schedule?

Having just been reminded of what I had seen taking place under the banner of the Church of Rome, I certainly did not feel like wasting precious time reading someone's experience of fifty years in the Church of Rome. My one day's involvement would last me a lifetime. The book was placed on my bookshelf along with many others, which I had not found time to read.

Amongst the other items which had been delivered by post that day was a newsletter which had been printed in Martinville, USA. the newsletter was entitled, *Heaven's Weapons*; and read as follows: 'St. Dominic was inspired by God to prophesy that one day the blessed Mother would give us devotions to be known as the Rosary and Scapular, through which she would save the world'.

'What utter nonsense!', I thought. Turning to Hebrews 10:12 and 1 John 1:7 my belief that Jesus Christ alone was sacrificed once for all was confirmed. This teaching was every bit as corrupt as the sacrament of penance practised and believed by some in the Philippines. It also denied the sufficiency of the sacrifice of Jesus.

On the same page was a picture of the Pope, hands clasped in prayer. The article running parallel to the photograph read: 'Pope John Paul II says that the Rosary which he prays daily is his favourite prayer. He urges all to pray it and understand the supreme role of devotion to Mary in the family theme, and the importance of the Rosary as a family devotion.'

I searched through the Bible but could find no scripture to substantiate the Pope's teaching on the Rosary as a family devotion. Mary was a special vessel unto the Lord. The angel of the Lord said of Mary:

> *'Thou are highly favoured, the Lord is with thee; blessed art thou among women'* (Luke 1:28)

Mary, the mother of Jesus' humanity said to the servants:

*'Whatsoever He saith unto you, do it.'* (John 2:5)

Nowhere in the Bible can we read that Mary gave guidance or instruction, except to say that we must do whatsoever Jesus said.

Mary said we are to do what Jesus said. Jesus did not give instruction that the Rosary was to be a family devotion. Jesus said:

*'In that day ye shall ask me nothing. Verily, verily I say unto you, whatsoever ye shall ask the Father in my name, He will give it you.'* (John 16:23)

Jesus has given us clear instructions how to pray; we are not to pray even to Him, but we are to pray to the Father in the name of Jesus. This is confirmed in 1 Timothy 2:5:

*'For there is one God, and one mediator between God and men, the man Christ Jesus.'*

Mary instructed that we are to do whatsoever Jesus saith. Jesus did not teach that we are to be devoted to Mary. Jesus taught:

*'Thou shalt love the Lord thy God with all thy heart, and with all thy soul and with all thy mind. This is the first and great commandment.'* (Matt 22:37–38)

Jesus came not to do His will or Mary's will. He came to do the will of the Father. He said of Himself:

*'I can of my own self do nothing, as I hear I judge, and my judgement is just, because I seek not mine own will,*

*but the will of the Father, which hath sent me.'* (John 5:30)

Oh how grieved Mary would be if she knew that men and women were walking in disobedience to Jesus' words, directing their devotions to her, instead of God, who alone is worthy of all praise and devotion. For God came in the form of the man, Christ Jesus, and died for the sins of mankind.

Having scriptural evidence that the Pope's teaching on praying the Rosary and devotions to Mary also denied the sufficiency of the sacrifice of Jesus, I was about to discard the newsletter in the waste paper bin when my eyes fixed on another heading.

# *Chapter 2*

# More than the Mother of Jesus

## 'Mary's Rosary Promises to St. Dominic'

Out of curiosity, I read on: 'Whoever shall faithfully pray my Rosary:

1. Shall have powerful armour against evil. It will destroy vice, decrease sin, defeat heretics.
2. Shall find it will cause virtue and good works to flourish.
3. Shall not perish.
4. Shall remain in the Grace of God and become worthy of eternal life.
5. Shall be delivered from purgatory.
6. Shall merit a high degree of glory in Heaven.'

I was dumbfounded; such teaching was total blasphemy. If Mary could have done all this, simply through Rosary prayers, why did Jesus have to suffer the agonies of crucifixion? Yes, there was only one word for such a teaching – **blasphemy**! It totally denied the sufficiency of the sacrifice of our Lord. If Mary knew, surely it would break her heart.

Not wanting my mind contaminated by such heresy I disposed of the newsletter in its rightful place – the dustbin; it was outrageous; an affront to the Holy Scriptures. A lot of good had crossed the

Atlantic from America; also a lot of evil. I comforted myself with the thought that the newsletter must have been written by some crank who was deeply involved in the occult.

I do not believe in strange coincidences; when we walk with the Lord and ask His guidance, He begins to direct our paths. Sometimes we are a little slow to recognise the hand of the Lord in the situation, especially if the outcome is different from what we expect.

Through the arrival of another unexpected and unusual newsletter through the letterbox within a matter of ten days, I began to recognise the hand of the Lord at work. The title of this most recent letter was 'Friends of Child Jesus'. This, I noted, was printed in Surrey, England, dated August 1986.

I read:

> 'This newsletter will tell you of the wonderful graces coming to England – and also to the whole world. I hope you will help Our Lady and Our Lord to realise the desire of their tender hearts – a wonderful new age of Innocence and Love'.
>
> 'Messages from Our Lady – April 14, 1986. Our Lady: "Oh my children I cannot tell you how urgently I come to you. The forces of evil gather for a great battle. Help me! My children, spread the devotion, help those poor people, helpless apostles as the children of God helped the first apostles.
>
> 'You all have become apostles of the new age of Innocence. Oh my children, this land for the church will be lost. Show heaven that you accept this gift of great mercy. Build the first church of the Triumphant Innocence in **this** country." '

May 8, 1986: Conversion of England: Our Lady: 'My children, I implore you to say the chaplet and the Holy Rosary, preparation must be made in **this** country. Defend yourselves with the daily Rosary. Increase its use in your homes. Where the Rosary is said, great protection will be yours.'

'I beg you, acquire this land, so that from this one centre of peace and reconciliation, thousands of crucified victims will find relief. This first shrine to the Triumphant Innocence will be the first of many, everywhere. The first church must be built here in England.'

'Will you reject this great grace? Those who help build whis shrine will be doing untold penance and make great reparation for their own sins and the sins of the world.'

July 11, 1986: Priest: 'Mother, this land is slipping from us. Help us! Some people say that this is not the place, that you, the Mother of God would choose. They say that such a large amount of money needed to offer the owners and builders could be given to the poor.'

Our Lady: 'My child, every penny that is given to "acquire the land" is given to the poor – the poor crucified victims of sin, weakness, disobedience, circumstances, history and pride.

'If every Catholic in this country gave one pound you would be well on the way to raising up a shrine to the crucified victims of the world. If every good soul of any race or religion, gave one pound, because they longed for peace, unity and love to reign in the world, there would be no strain on a single person to acquire the land and build the first shrine in the world. Let this tiny piece of England, where once there was a house of prayer, say "Yes" unto the desire of heaven.

Give what you can to help build this little shrine. In helping to bring about this miracle of love and unity, Christian, Jews, Muslims, Hindus, all races and all peoples will be standing up to say "No" to the wicked, the greedy, the oppressed and "Yes" to love, peace and harmony.'

'This message and others regarding the shrine should go out all over the world. Heaven appeals to the children of men. You are one family. You are brothers and sisters. Help and love each other. This little piece of land will be lost if you do not act quickly. This is Heaven's desire. Will you allow it to come to nothing through your complacency? The choice is yours.

"I have wept and pleaded with millions of mothers and suffering souls; have pity and help. **Let this church that was once demolished** be rebuilt as a symbol of the resurrection and beginning of a New Age of Innocence, love and peace. The chains around the gates must be broken by a spirit of love (the gates of the side of the shrine are fastened with chains)." '

July 5 1986: Our Lady: 'Please my children help me to raise up the first church of the Triumphant Innocence on this soil. Raise what is needed to acquire the land. Use every way open to you. England has been given great grace from Heaven. Those who give even the smallest help in building this church will have their names written in the Eucharistic Hearts of Jesus and Mary. Many, many sins will be forgiven; many infidelities forgotten, even though their sins are as scarlet. Come to the source of all forgiveness – the sacrament of penance.

Benediction: '. . . At the Prayer for England, blood burst from the Host and Our Lord said, "England, my heart bleeds for you. Make reparation . . .

England, do penance, make reparation for this. My Mother pleads for you yet you shame her with this title *The Abortion Centre of the Word*. She wishes you to remember that you are her dowry. You were once called the Island of Saints".'

Look at these messages carefully and take note. Can they be made up by this poor instrument?'

It can't be true! It can't be true! . . . were the only words which I seemed to be able to utter during the reading of the article. I was shocked! I wandered around the room in a daze. My heart felt as though it was five times its normal size and was beating so hard it felt as though it might burst any second.

Going to my bedroom I shut and locked the door. I needed to talk to my Father in Heaven, but my burden was too great for mere words. I wept, groaned and cried uncontrollably, until my body was drained of all strength, my stomach ached and felt as though it had been turned inside out.

With the Psalmist, I cried unto the Lord:

*'Give ears to my prayer, O God, and hide not thyself from my supplication. Attend unto me and hear me. I moan in my complaint and make a noise.*

*Because of the voice of the enemy, because of the oppression of the wicked my heart is sore pained within me and the terrors of death are fallen upon me.*

*Fearfulness and trembling are come upon me and horror has overwhelmed me.*

*And I said, Oh that I had the wings of a dove, for then would I fly away, and be at rest.*

*Lo, then would I wander far off and remain in the wilderness. I would hasten my escape from the windy storm and tempest.* (Psalm 55:1–8)

When not wanting to face danger the ostrich hides his head in the sand. At that moment I wished I could hide my head in the sand, or fly to some remote island and pretend that the rest of the world did not exist. Yet I knew if I were to remain obedient to the leading of the Lord, I must be willing to face the enemy, head on.

The desire of my heart was for the Lord to comfort me and say, 'there, there my child, you are overreacting and your fears are unfounded'. No such words of comfort were forthcoming from the Lord.

The pain and unrest in my heart continued until I became willing to face the truth. The newsletter had been positive proof that the abominable doctrines of the sacrament of penance and praying the Rosary were not unique to the Philippines and Spain. These doctrines of devils were also practiced in America and Britain. Granted, the penances in America and Britain were not so barbaric as those practiced in the Philippines.

On reflection, I wonder if that is right. The self flagellation practiced in the Philippines harmed only those who chose to punish themselves. The money given by deluded souls as a penance for sin in Britain would be used to further the work of building the Apostate Church and lead enquiring sinners into further deception.

In whatever form it is practiced, the doctrine of penance can not be substantiated by the Holy Scriptures. It is an evil doctrine that denies the sufficiency of the sacrifice of Jesus and the gospel of grace. What fellowship can light and darkness have? It is no part of the Christian gospel.

# Chapter 3

# Justification by Faith

Some may boast self-flagellation and 24 lashes, others of their devotions to Mary, and Rosary prayers. Still others may boast of the money they have given and indulgences received; while others boast of what they have sacrificed and given up, in an attempt to please God.

According to the Holy Scriptures:

> *'. . . ye were not redeemed with corruptible things, as silver and gold, from your vain conversations received by tradition from your fathers;*
>
> *But with the precious blood of Christ as a lamb without blemish and without spot'.* (1 Peter 1:18–19)

Therefore, no amount of penances, praying the Rosary, giving of money, sacrifices or good works, can save us from the wrath of God or cleanse us from sin.

> *'For by grace are ye saved, through faith; and not of yourselves: it is a gift of God: Not of works, lest any man should boast.'* (Ephesians 2:8–9)

God despises every human effort done in man's own strength as a means of obtaining salvation or favours with Him. Why? Because He will not assist a thief, who tries to climb in any other way than the way He has opened. Jesus said:

> *'I am the door: by me, if any man enter in, he shall be saved . . .'* (John 10:9)

At some stage in our Christian walk, most of us have cried out to God in desperation because of our failures, 'Oh God, don't you see how hard I am trying to be holy? Lord, you have said in your word, ***"Be ye holy for I am holy"***. Lord, I have failed you again. I am a miserable failure, help me. Nothing is impossible with you!'

We assume that our Heavenly Father is pleased with our struggles as we strive to walk in obedience to His word and be holy; yet, this means of "trying to be holy" is attempting to climb in through a door other than the door that was opened for us, trying to establish our own righteousness, through lack of knowledge.

> *'For I bear them record that they have a zeal of God, but not according to knowledge.*
>
> *For they, being ignorant of God's righteousness, and going about to establish their own righteousness, have not submitted themelves unto the righteousness of God, for Christ is the end of the law for righteousness to everyone that believeth.'* (Romans 10:2–4)

God is not interested in helping us to patch up our weak spots. He wants to exchange our filthy rags of selfrighteousness with the robe of Christ's righteousness, so that we may be . . .

> *'. . . found in Him, not having mine own righteousness, which is of the law, but that which is through the faith of Christ, the righteousness which is of God by faith':*
>
> (Phil 3:9)

*'There is none righteous, no, not one':* (Romans 3:10)

We have all sinned and fallen short of God's holiness. To be holy, as He is holy, we must totally submit to the righteousness of Christ through faith alone. This can only be achieved by confessing before the throne of grace that our own futile efforts of attempting to walk in holiness have been hopeless. We must humble ourselves before the mighty hand of God, confessing we are weak, sinful, sensuous; and that in our flesh dwelleth no good thing. For we are poor, wretched, weak and totally helpless lumps of clay, totally dependent on the righteousness of Christ which is the free gift of God through faith.

Concerning justification by faith, Dr David Samuel has written, 'The doctrine of justification by faith must have a place of primary significance . . . because experientially it must be at the centre of our relationship with God. I am puzzled by Christians who say, "Yes we understand the teaching about justification by faith, but now we want to pass on to other things." That indicates to me that they have not understood.

Justification by faith is not a ladder that I climb up, to get where I want to be, and then can kick away. The right image is not of a ladder, but of a life belt that keeps me afloat every moment and of which I cannot let go without drowning. Justification is not something merely for the beginning of the Christian life, after which we pass onto other things, for the just shall live by faith. What is the life of faith if it is not "simul peccator et justus" at one and the same time sinful and righteous – sinful in myself, righteous in Christ, mourning in myself, rejoicing in the Lord. Every moment of my existence I depend on the righteousness of Christ to keep me in existence before God.'

*'The life which I now live in the flesh, I live by the faith of the Son of God, who loved me and gave himself for me.'* (Gal 2:20)

Justification by faith is central to the whole of the Christian's life and experience. It is not something he transcends, moves on from, leaves behind in his experience; the moment he talks like that he shows that he does not understand what justification by faith is. So rightly understood, justification by faith is of essential and abiding importance both for the Church and for the individual Christian, and if we lose sight of that fact and fail to appropriate it, the doctrine of justification is already imperilled.

'To justify' in scripture means 'to declare or to pronounce righteous'. It was a serious mistake in the Vulgate that the term should have been translated by the Latin word 'justificate' which means 'to make righteous'. In the Bible, 'to justify' is a legal term associated with the law courts. The prisoner stands in the court, the evidence is heard and the judge pronounces the verdict. In pronouncing the verdict the judge does not make or unmake the moral character and condition of the defendant, he merely declares him just or guilty. This is shown clearly in Deuteronomy 25:1:

*'If there be a controversy between men, and they come unto a judgement, that the judges may judge them, then they shall justify the righteous and condemn the wicked'.*

Whereas the term 'to justify' is used with reference to our acceptance with God, it means 'to declare a person just' it does not mean 'to make just'. God justifies us freely by His grace (Rom 3:24); therefore justification has nothing to do with goodness on our part or with our moral or spiritual condition.

*'Therefore being justified by faith, we have peace with God through our Lord Jesus Christ.'* (Romans 5:1)

*'For we which have believed do enter into rest.'*
(Hebrews 4:3)

We who truly believe the gospel can live in absolute peace and joy, resting upon the righteousness of Christ 'by faith'. Being holy as He is holy – **by faith alone**.

# *Chapter 4*

# Purgatory versus Heaven or Hell

During the reading of the two newsletters mentioned in a previous chapter, I had come across a few words that were unfamiliar to me. These were 'purgatory', 'mortal sin', 'the Host', 'indulgences' and 'the Scapular'.

Being of an inquisitive nature, I decided to find out what these words meant. My complete concordance to the New and Old Testaments revealed that not one of these words were to be found in the Bible.

Turning to the dictionary, I found the meaning of the word 'purgatory': 'tending to cleanse, cleansing; according to Roman Catholics and others, a place in which souls, after death, are purified from venial sins and suffer punishment for mortal sins, not atoned for.'

As far as I was aware through my understanding of Scripture, sin was sin. There were neither little nor big sins, for those who believed the gospel, the blood of Jesus cleansed us of all sin.

What do Roman Catholics believe the difference is between venial and mortal sin, I wondered? The dictionary was once again my source of information:

'Venial . . . that may be forgiven; pardonable; not deeply sinful; excusable.'

'Mortal sin . . . incurring the penalty of death; or divine condemnation.'

If my conclusion was right, purgatory, according to Roman Catholics, was a place where souls after death are purified of excusable sins and suffer punishment for sins which were looked upon as worthy of divine condemnation. Could this teaching in any way be justified by the written word of God? I set about the task of studying the Bible to find the answer.

The apostle Paul, formerly known as Saul (Acts 13:9), had much for which he needed forgiveness. Before he became a follower of the Lord Jesus he was guilty of the most dreadful persecution of the Lord's disciples.

> *'Which thing I also did in Jerusalem: and many of the saints did I shut up in prison, having received authority from the chief priests; and when they were put to death I gave my voice against them.*
>
> *And I punished them oft in every synagogue, and compelled them to blaspheme; and being exceedingly mad against them, I persecuted them even unto strange cities.'*
>
> (Acts 26:10–11)

Did the apostle Paul believe that his soul would go to purgatory to be purified of venial sins and suffer punishment for mortal sins? . . . for his sins were many! Even after many years of serving the Lord, Paul wrote:

> *'For I know that in me (that is my flesh) dwelleth no good thing; for to will is present with me; but to perform that which is good I find not. For the good that I would, I do not; but the evil which I would not, that I do.'*
>
> (Romans 7:18–19)

Here Paul acknowledges that he is far from perfect. His intention and urge was always to do that which was right. Yet there was another law in his members, warring against the law of his mind (his new nature) which on occasion stopped him doing the good he wanted to do. For the flesh serves the law and sin. *The flesh lusteth against the Spirit and the Spirit against the flesh and these are contrary the one to the other, so that ye cannot do the things that ye would.*

The new nature cannot commit sin! (1 John 3:9) But the unregenerate part, the flesh, constantly works towards sin. Even where there is new life in Christ through the indwelling of the Holy Spirit, there are remnants of carnal affections. Therefore we cannot attain to sinless perfection in this life. In verse seventeen of Romans chapter seven, Paul states:

*'Now then, it is no more I that do it, but sin that dwelleth in me.'*

This was not an excuse for the guilt of sin that burdened him, but, that he might take comfort from the covenant of grace, which accepts the willingness of spirit, and provides pardon for the weakness of the flesh, which he was constantly striving against. He cried out:

*'O wretched man that I am, who shall deliver me from the body of this death?'* (Romans 7:24)

Did his hope of deliverance lie in suffering in purgatory? No! His hope was in Jesus.

*'I thank my God, through Jesus Christ our Lord'* (v 25)

If not for Jesus this iniquity which dwells within us all would certainly be our ruin.

Why did Paul make no mention of finding his way to heaven by suffering for his sins in purgatory? Simply because he believed the gospel of Jesus Christ, he knew that Jesus bore the punishment for his sins. In the letter to the Galatians, he wrote:

*'I do not frustrate the grace of God, for if righteousness came by the law, then CHRIST IS DEAD IN VAIN.'*
(Galatians 2:21)

In other words, 'works' frustrate the gospel of God and the death of Jesus Christ. If righteousness and salvation came by the law of Moses and the law of suffering in purgatory, then Christ died in vain.

*'. . . Christ also hath ONCE suffered for sins, the just for the unjust, that he might bring us to God, being put to death in the flesh, but quickened in the Spirit.'*
(1 Peter 3:18)

The above scripture needs no further explanation and is confirmed in the Epistle to the Hebrews:

*'For by ONE offering He hath perfected forever, them that are sanctified.'* (Heb 10:14)

Jesus said:

*'Verily, verily, I say unto you, He that believeth my words and believeth on him that sent me, hath everlasting life, and shall NOT come into condemnation; but is passed from death unto life.'* (John 5:24)

## The Place Called Hell

'God is too good to send anyone to Hell' is the main argument raised against Hell today. I must agree with those who follow this line of thinking – God is too good to send anyone to Hell. God does not send people to Hell; He has provided a way of escape. People send themselves to Hell by rejecting His **ONLY** way of salvation.

*'The gift of God is eternal life through Jesus Christ.'*
(Romans 6:23)

*'Neither is there salvation in any other; for there is NONE other name under Heaven given amongst men, whereby we must be saved.'* (Acts 4:12)

All who reject God's plan of salvation through Jesus Christ will go to Hell. People do not go to Hell for smoking, drinking or telling lies. People go to Hell because they do not repent of their sins and accept Jesus as their Saviour.

*'There was a certain rich man, who was clothed in purple and fine linen, and fared sumptuously every day. And there was a certain beggar named Lazarus, which was laid at his gate, full of sores, and desiring to be fed with the crumbs which fell from the rich man's table: moreover, the dogs came and licked his sores.*

*And it came to pass that the beggar died and was carried by the angels into Abraham's bosom: the rich man also died, and was buried; and in Hell he lifted up his eyes, being in torments and seeth Abraham afar off, and Lazarus in his bosom.*

*And he cried and said,*

*"Father Abraham have mercy on me and send Lazarus that he might dip the tip of his finger in water, and cool my tongue; for I am tormented in this flame".'*
(Luke 16:19–24)

The Lord's revelation regarding the rich man and

Lazarus in Hell helps us to understand that in Old Testament days, and in the days during the Lord's ministry on earth, the spirits of the dead departed to a place called Hell or 'Sheol' in the Hebrew and 'Hades' in the Greek. For clarity we will use the Greek translation 'Hades'.

Hades was divided into two compartments. The spirits of the Old Testament saints, who had remained faithful to the Old Covenant, and the spirits of those who were saved and had died during the Lord's ministry on earth went to the compartment named 'Abraham's Bosom', which was a place of comfort. The spirits of all who had rejected the Old Covenant and salvation through Jesus during His ministry on earth, went to a place of torment.

> ' " *. . . send Lazarus that he may dip the tip of his finger in water and cool my tongue, for I am tormented in this flame.*" ' (Luke 16:24)

It was impossible for Lazarus to help the rich man in his suffering and pain:

> ' . . . "*Between us and you there is a great gulf fixed, so that they which would pass from hence to you cannot; neither can they pass to us, that would come from thence.*" ' (Luke 16:26)

There is no means of escape, no second chance – the great gulf is fixed.

Jesus' spirit went to Hell (Hades) when he died on the cross.

> '*For thou wilt not leave my soul in hell, neither wilt thou suffer thine Holy One to see corruption*'.
>
> (Psalm 16:10 & Acts 2:31)

The Lord spent three days and three nights in Hades which is situated in the heart of the earth.

'. . . *so shall the Son of Man be three days and three nights in the heart of the earth.*' (Matt 12:40)

Jesus and the repentant thief did not go to the place of torment but to Abraham's Bosom, which is here called Paradise.

'*Today shalt thou be with me in Paradise*' (Luke 23:43)

After his death Jesus **first** descended into the lower parts of the earth, then He ascended upon high. When he ascended upon high he led captivity captive, in other words, he led a multitude of captives (see Ephesians 4:8–10). A great change took place in Hades after the Lord's Ascension. He led the captives of Abraham's bosom home to Heaven. Since the moment of the Lord's ascension into Heaven the spirits of the righteous dead go directly to Heaven.

Paul makes it quite clear that the spirits of the righteous dead no longer go to Abraham's bosom, he tell us:

'*To be absent from the body and to be present with the Lord.*' (2 Corinthians 5:8)

Paul desired to:

'*Depart, and to be with Christ*' (Philippians 1:23)

Abraham's Bosom became redundant nearly two thousand years ago. The spirits of all who have died in Christ since His ascension immediately go to be with the Lord, and we know where He is:

'. . . *He was received up into heaven and sat on the right hand of God.*' (Mark 16:19)

Hades, the place of torment, still remains the abode for spirits of the unsaved, and will continue to be so until one thousand years after the second coming of Jesus, when . . .

'. . . *death (the grave) and hell (Hades) were cast into the lake of fire.*' (Revelation 20:14)

We know of course that death holds the bodies of the dead and Hades hold the spirits of the wicked dead. None of the wicked will be forgotten; they will be resurrected to stand before the great white judgement throne of God.

'*And whosoever was not found written in the book of life, was cast into the lake of fire.*' (Revelation 20:15)

The lake of fire is the final Hell and eternal abode for the unsaved. There they will join the Beast and the False Prophet and spend eternity in the presence of Satan and his fallen angels to be tormented day and night for ever and ever. (Revelation 20:10).

My examination of the word of God proved that the doctrine of purgatory cannot be substantiated by the Holy Scriptures. What motivated Rome into inventing such a doctrine, I mused? I found the answer in the pages of Charles Chiniquy's book, '50 years in the Church of Rome'. Much of Rome's wealth is a result of money paid by poor, grief stricken widows, who believe they have to pay the priests money to sing special prayers, which reduce the length of time that their departed ones will have to suffer in the purifying flame of purgatory.

Charles cried out, 'How long, O Lord, shall that insolent enemy of the gospel, the Church of Rome, fatten herself upon the tears of the widow and orphan, with that cruel, pagan invention, purgatory? Oh, remove the veil from the eyes of the priests and people of Rome, as thou hast removed it from mine! Make them understand that their hopes of purification must not rest on these fires, but only on the blood of the lamb, shed on Calvary, to save the world'.

## The Host, The Mass and Transubstantiation

The bread, or wafer, used in the Mass is called 'the Host'. When the Host has been consecrated and offered up as a sacrifice in the Mass it then becomes the Eucharist. It is believed that the prayer of consecration over the bread and wine causes the substance of the bread and wine to change into the substance of the actual body, blood, soul and divinity of Jesus, while the outward appearance remains the same. Only the priests partake of the body and blood, while their followers partake of the body only.

The Pope's followers believe that the bread or Host consecrated in the Mass 'becomes' Jesus Christ. When they swallow the wafer they believe they have taken full possession of Jesus Christ, not in a symbolical way, but that they are swallowing His soul, divinity, His flesh, His bones, His head,

His feet, His whole body. If they do not believe this they are told that they shall be damned forever.

What an absolutely abhorrent thought! To think of our Holy Saviour, the Creator of the World, being eaten by millions of His created ones daily in the sacrament of Mass. Surely such teaching must have been instigated by Satan, the arch enemy of God. Yet the Roman Catholic Canon states:

> 'If anyone shall deny that the Body and the Blood, together with the Soul and Divinity of our Lord Jesus Christ, and therefore entire Christ, are truly and substantially contained in the sacrament of the most Holy Eucharist, and say that He is only in it as a figure, let him be accursed.' (damned, or under a curse).

If not for my in-depth study into the doctrine of Catholicism, I would not have understood what the Roman Catholic Church actually believes and teaches on the subject of 'transubstantiation'. I have come to realise that very few Catholics actually realise what they are taking part in when they celebrate the Mass. From early childhood the priest places the wafer on their tongue and declares 'this is the body of Christ'. It became such a natural and normal way of life that their minds never questioned the fact that they had Jesus Christ in their mouths, though this is exactly what transubstantiation means.

According to Roman Catholic irreversible church decree (named dogma), they teach that their priests are the only ones who have the authority from God to pronounce the blessing which changes the elements of bread and wine into the actual body and blood of Jesus; therefore they are the only church where Jesus physically resides, even today. They believe and teach that the Roman Catholic Church was founded by Jesus Christ when He was here on earth. It is the 'only' church founded by Jesus. The greatest asset of their church is that they have Jesus 'present' in the Holy Eucharist. Anyone who does not hold to this belief, in the most explicit details, is accursed and damned forever.

The teaching of transubstantiation does not date back to the Last Supper as most of the Pope's followers are taught to believe. It was a controversial subject for many centuries before becoming an article of faith (which means 'essential to salvation' according to Rome). It was not until the fourth Lateran Council in 1215 AD that it was officially defined and canonized as a dogma by Pope Innocent III.

Catholic Canon VI:

> 'If anyone shall say that Christ the only begotten Son of God is not to be adored "in the Holy Sacrament of the Eucharist" and that he is not to be publicly set before the people to be adored, and that his adorers are idolators, let him be accursed.'

In many Masses even today, after the bread has been supposedly changed through transubstantiation by the prayer of consecration into the blood, body, soul and divinity of Christ, it is placed in a holder called a monstrance; the priest stands before the assembled company holding the monstrance in a position where it can be seen by the crowd, who bow before it, adore it and worship it as God. Sometimes they have processions where they solemnly march, as the congregation bows and offers praise, worship and adoration – to a piece of bread.

These Canon Laws are still in effect today. As the Second Vatican Council commenced in 1963, Pope John XXXIII declared:

> 'I do accept entirely all that has been decided and declared at the Council of Trent.'

What exactly did the Council of Trent decide and declare? The previous two Canon statements include the following, plus many more, which are equally as blasphemous:

> 'If any one will say that in these words "this do ye in remembrance of me" Christ did not make the apostles and priests or did not ordain that they themselves and other priests should offer His Body and Blood let him be anathema (cursed).
>
> If anyone shall say that the sacrifice of the mass is only of praise and thanksgiving, or a bare commendation of the sacrifice performed on the cross, but not propitiatary, as that is of benefit only to the person that takes it, and ought not to be offered for the living and the dead for sins, punishments, satisfactions and other necessities, let him be accursed.'

The same Canon Laws are still in effect today. Many are expressing hope that Rome is turning to a scriptural Christianity, and point to the many reforms of Vatican II, and the ever widening charismatic renewal. However, they fail to realise that these changes are only superficial, a smokescreen to cover up their true intentions.

If Rome renounces her doctrines of transubstantiation, penances, purgatory, worship of the Hosts, worship of Mary that is due to Jesus, superstitious crucifixes, Rosary beads and much more, then and only then, should we believe she is beginning to change. I doubt very much if this could ever happen for the Pope would have to admit that he is not infallible, that he is not perfectly reliable and just as capable of falling into error as any other human being on the face of this earth.

The infallible Pope of the sixteenth century gave the order to execute, by burning alive, those who refused to accept his doctrine of transubstantiation. Bible-believing Christians were tied to posts, a bonfire of dried brushwood was piled around them. If they refused to confess that in the wafer (Host) was the actual blood, body, soul and divinity of Jesus Christ, the brushwood was set alight. As the flames engulfed the victims the priests of Roman brandished their crucifixes and proclaimed, 'All this is done for the greater glory of God!'

I feel more sorry for the priests than the Bible-believing Christians who remained faithful to the gospel, even unto death. They knew they were going to 'be with Christ'; their suffering for the gospel's sake was over.

What about the poor, deceived priests who were willing to commit murder for the traditions of mere men? Unless they repented and renounced the Roman Catholic religion and its heretical doctrines, they will now be being punished for their sins in that place called Hell.

Did the apostle Paul teach that the bread actually 'became' Jesus Christ? Absolutely not! He delivered unto the Corinthians exactly what he received from the Lord concerning the bread and wine.

*'Take, eat, this is my body which is broken for you; this do in REMEMBRANCE OF ME.*

*After the same manner also he took the cup, when he had supped saying, "This cup is the new testament (covenant) in my blood: this do you, as oft as ye drink it, in REMEMBRANCE OF ME."'*

(1 Corinthians 11:24–25)

We may have been shocked by the 'let them be accursed' threats of the Council of Trent. Let those who stand against the truth of God's Word know, those curses will fall back on their own heads, for the words of the apostle Paul call out across the centuries:

*'But though we, or an angel from heaven, preach any other gospel unto you than that which we have preached unto you, let him be accursed.'* (Galatians 1:8)

Not only does Paul warn that an authentic angel should not be heeded while preaching a 'different doctrine'; Paul strictly warned the Galatians not to even listen to him, if he were to change any of the fundemental teachings of the gospel. How much more then should we reject the traditions and practices of a religion that is not only unbiblical, but is actually steeped in occult practices.

## The Lord's Supper or Communion

Our Saviour said:

*'Ye shall know the truth, and the truth shall make you free.'* (John 8:32)

The Word of God reveals the truth to us concerning the Lord's Supper.

*'With desire I have desired to eat this "passover" with you before I suffer.'* (Luke 22:15)

The word 'passover' comes from the Hebrew word 'pasach' which signifies 'to pass or leap over'. The name 'passover' was given to the feast which was established in commemoration of the coming forth out of Egypt. The evening before the passover the Israelites killed a lamb, the lamb was roasted and then eaten; the blood was smeared on the door-posts of the homes in which the lamb was eaten. The night before their departure the destroying angel slew the first born of the Egyptians but passed over the Israelites because of the blood of the lamb on the doorposts. See Exodus 12:7–13.

And the Lord said:

*'And this day shall be unto you for a memorial and ye shall keep it a feast to the LORD throughout the generations; ye shall keep it as a feast by an ordinance forever.'*
(Exodus 12:14)

The Jewish Feast of the Passover was celebrated as a memorial of this coming forth out of Egypt throughout the generations, and was also celebrated by Jesus, for he desired to celebrate the commemoration of the Passover with his disciples before He himself suffered and was sacrificed for us. It was the last Passover Jesus would celebrate until the marriage feast (see Rev 19:7) when the Kingdom of God shall come.

Jesus had fellowshipped with his disciples and eaten the Passover lamb, then He gave them the fruit of the vine which they were to drink 'in remembrance' of the blood of the lamb that was sacrificed and smeared on the doorposts to save the Israelites from the wrath of the destroying angel. They did not drink the actual blood of the lamb, they drank the fruit of the vine 'in remembrance' of the deliverance out of Egypt.

The passover and deliverance out of Egypt were typical and prophetic signs of the Christ to come, who should by dying, deliver us from sin, the tyranny of Satan, and death.

Jesus was our Passover Lamb.

> '. . .*For even Christ our passover is sacrificed for us'*
> (1 Corinthians 5:7)

Now and from henceforth it is the New Covenant in His blood – no more the lamb's body, but His body, His blood. He took the bread and gave thanks, and broke it and gave unto them saying:

> *'This is my body which is given for you; do this in remembrance of me.'* (Luke 22:19)

The disciples knew that the bread had not 'become' the Lord's body for Jesus was standing right there in front of them. He was showing them how the Passover Feast of the New Covenant was to be celebrated, and in so doing was explaining to them that His hour of suffering for the sins of the world had come. He was about to give His body over to be scourged (beaten, lashed, broken) and nailed to a tree for them, and us.

Having celebrated the commemoration of the first Passover Lamb, they knew exactly what Jesus meant when he said,

> *'This is my body which is given for you, do this in remembrance of me.'* (Luke 22:19)

It would be absolutely ludicrous to think that the disciples would, even for a moment, have considered cooking, then eating, the Lord's body in the same manner as had been practised after the sacrifice of the first Passover lamb. The doctrine of transubstantiation practised by Rome is as ludicrous as the previous statement.

*Jesus then took the cup and said, 'This cup is the New Testament in my blood, which is shed for you.'*

(Luke 22:20)

In the first three Gospels Jesus said:

*'I will not drink of this "fruit of the vine" till I drink it new with you in my Father's Kingdom.'*

The Lord's disciples were to drink of the fruit of the vine, in remembrance of His blood that was about to be poured out from them.

*'One of the soldiers with a spear pierced His side, and forthwith come there out blood and water.'* (John 19:34)

We must remember the disciples were in the habit of drinking of the fruit of the vine in commemoration of the blood of the first passover lamb. They positively and sincerely understood that the wine in the cup had not 'become' the blood of Christ, but was representative of His blood.

*'For as often as you eat this bread* (not body) *and drink this cup* (fruit of the vine, not blood) *ye shew forth the Lord's death till He come.'*

(1 Corinthians 11:26 (author's paraphrase))

Where then did the doctrine of the celebration of the Mass, as practised by Rome come from? Not the

Holy Scriptures! It was the invention of one who lost his faith of Hope. As the Lord tarried, he substituted the truth for something which would make Jesus 'seem' real, and appear to be present.

## The Sacrifice of the Mass

Why do we see Jesus still upon the cross in Catholic Churches? According to the Church of Rome's teaching Jesus is 'still' dying for the sins of the world.

The Mass is the same as the sacrifice of the cross. No matter how many times it is offered or in how many places at one time, it is the same sacrifice of Christ. Christ is forever offering himself in the mass.

On the cross Jesus cried, ***'It is finished'***. He had fulfilled His mission; our precious Lord's suffering on earth was finally over. In spite of the fact that He had lived a perfect life before God and man, He had been rejected, laughed at, spat upon, beaten beyond recognition and finally nailed to a cross. He had endured willingly to pay the penalty for the sins of the world – past, present and future, **once** for all.

The words 'it is finished' have been interpreted by a priest of Rome to mean that He had finished His formal, normal, earthly life and was now 'fixed in the state of a victim' . . . He had begun His everlasting career as the 'perpetual sacrifice' of the new law. Every crucifix with Jesus portrayed as nailed to it, tells the lie that Jesus is perpetually dying for sins.

Thank God for the truth that is found in His Word.

*'Wherefore he is able also to save them to the uttermost that come unto God by Him, seeing that he ever LIVETH to make intercession for them'* (Hebrews 7:25)

Who dares to oppose the Word of the living God, who said of Himself?:

*'I am He that liveth and was dead; and behold, I am alive for evermore, Amen; and have the keys of hell and death.'* (Revelation 1:18)

The Bible clearly and repeatedly affirms in the most positive terms that Jesus' sacrifice on Calvary was complete in that one offering. Also that it was never to be repeated is set forth explicitly in Hebrews Chapters 7, 9 & 10.

*'Who needeth not daily, as those high priests, to offer up sacrifice, first for their own sins, and then for the people's: for this He did once, when He offered up Himself.'* (Hebrews 7:27)

*' . . . but by His own blood he entered in once into the holy place, having obtained eternal redemption for us.'* (Hebrews 9:12)

*'Nor yet that he should offer himself often . . . but now once in the end of the world hath he appeared to put away sin by the sacrifice of Himself . . . so Christ was once offered to bear the sins of many: and unto them that look for him shall he appear the second time without sin unto salvation.'* (Hebrews 9:25–28)

*' . . . we are sanctified through the offering of the body of Jesus Christ once for all.'* (Hebrews 10:10)

*' . . . for by one offering he hath perfected forever them that are sanctified'* (Hebrews 10:14)

All who say 'No' to the truth and continue in this pretence of a continuous offering for sin through the sacrifice of the Mass, continue to deny the sufficiency of the sacrifice of Jesus. Every one of Rome's doctrines that we have so far examined cause the Lord's death to be in vain. Surely the spirit behind such heresies is that of antichrist.

> *'Ye cannot drink of the cup of the Lord, and the cup of devils; ye cannot be partakers of the Lord's table, and the table of devils. Do we provoke the Lord to jealousy? Are we stronger than He?'* (1 Corinthians 10:21–22)

To partake of the Lord's supper is to profess that we believe by faith in the full sufficiency of Jesus' 'once and for all' sacrifice.

If we have communion with idolators or their heathen sacrifices we become partakers with them in their idolatry. It is a virtual renouncing of true Christianity to have communion with both Christ and devils. One must be renounced if the other is to be maintained, but you cannot be partakers of both.

Within the Ecumenical Charismatic Renewal Movement, people of all denominations are being encouraged to share in the unholy sacrifice of Mass. Those who fellowship with other gods provoke God to jealousy, for He is a jealous God. It is a dangerous thing to provoke God's anger unless we can withstand His power. Are we a match for God? Shall we cause almighty wrath by continuing to feast on the heathen sacrifice of the Host – the supposed actual body, blood, soul and divinity of Christ? Multitudes of people are bound to Rome through fear, fear of going against the Church lest they be damned. It is much wiser to fear God rather than man for:

> *'the fear of the Lord is the beginning of wisdom'*
> (Proverbs 9:10)

# *Chapter 5*

# In Rememberance and Memorial of Him

The Lord's Supper or Passover of the New Covenant is not merely a feast of remembrance, it is also a memorial, which serves to perpetuate the memory of all that Jesus accomplished for us through his suffering and the wonders of God's grace towards us, until Jesus comes.

Our walk with God as His covenant people is a walk of faith; for the just shall live by faith. Faith in the Word of God which declares the 'once and for all' sacrifice of the Lamb of God.

Why did Jesus give His body over to be scourged (brutally beaten with an instrument of torture)? His body was broken so that we could be healed:

> *' . . . by whose stripes (lashes) ye were healed.'*
>
> (1 Peter 2:24)

As we partake of the bread in the Passover feast of the New Covenant, it must be an act of faith, sincerely believing without any doubt, that Christ, our Passover Lamb's body, was lashed so that we could be healed. Christ our Passover lamb . . .

> '. . . *borne our griefs* (Hebrew translation "Choli" = sicknesses) *and carried our sorrows* (Hebrew "Makob" = pains) . . . *with his stripes we are healed.'*
>
> (Isaiah 53:4–5 (author's paraphrase))

The act of partaking of the bread, in complete

faith discerning the Lord's Body, enables us by the grace of God, to walk in divine health and glorify God in our bodies, which are the temple of the Holy Spirit.

Even in the midst of physical persecution, trust in the stripes of our Passover Lamb moves God with great compassion, as the apostle Paul's testimony proves. He was lashed thirty nine times on five different occasions, beaten with rods three times and stoned once. By the grace of God and faith in his Passover Lamb, he was able to write and tell Timothy:

> '. . . *what persecutions I endured: but out of THEM ALL the Lord delivered me*' (2 Timothy 3:11)

So whatever Satan seeks to lay at our door, whether sickness, disease, persecutions, afflictions, we can be confident that God's grace will be sufficient for us as we reach out in faith to our Passover Lamb, whose body was broken so that we could be healed.

Paul was finally beheaded, but through faith in his Lord, the enemy was unable to put an end to his life before he had fulfilled all that God had called him to. Paul had no fear of death; death to the true Christian is the door into glory to be 'with Christ'.

As we partake of the cup of the Passover Feast of the New Covenant, we humble ourselves before God and remember:

> '. . . *He hath made Him to be sin for us, who knew no sin; that we might be made the righteousness of God in Him*' (2 Corinthians 5:21)

Our Passover Lamb was sinless; he had no sin of His own, yet he was 'made' sin for us. His body became a sin offering, a sacrifice for sin, so that we who have no righteousness of our own, are made the righteousness of God in Him.

*'Who his own self bare our sins in his own body on the tree that we, being dead to sin, should live unto righteousness . . .'* (1 Peter 2:24)

As He hung on that tree, He bore our sins as the sacrificial Lamb of God, the sin offering that took away the sins of the world, so that all who would believe on His 'once and for all' sacrifice would be made the righteousness of God in Him.

As we lift the cup of the Passover feast to our lips we remember His Blood which was poured out for us, knowing, by faith, that the fruit of Christ's suffering was our sanctification and justification.

*'For God so loved the world, that he gave his only begotten son, that whosoever believeth in him should not perish, but have everlasting life.'* (John 3:16)

## Rome's Revelations

*'But in vain they do worship me, teaching for doctrines the commandments of men'* (Matt 15:9)

True born again Christians accept the 66 books of the Holy Bible as the sole and final revelation for salvation, faith and practise. They believe that supernatural revelation ended with the last verse of Revelation chapter 22; that anything added since then is false and contrary to the plain warning:

*'For I testify unto every man that heareth the words of the prophecy of this book, if any man shall add unto these things, God shall add unto him the plagues that are written in this book.'* (Rev 22:18)

Although the Church of Rome accepts the Bible as God's revelation and claims adherance to it, she violates it at every turn. Revelation according to Rome is the Bible plus the Apocryphal books, plus Tradition, plus the decisions of the Church Councils, plus the decrees of the infallible Popes, when they speak from their throne as head of the one true Church.

The majority of her Church doctrines are nowhere to be found in the Bible, but are additions which have been added over the centuries through decisions of mortal men.

Let us take a look at some, and here are only a few examples of Rome's revelations that have been added over the centuries.

The daily Mass was adopted in 394 AD.

The Doctrine of Purgatory was invented and put into practice in 593 AD.

Pope Boniface was the first Pope 610 AD.

The temporal powers of the Pope were declared in 750 AD.

Veneration of St Joseph began in 890 AD.

Canonization of dead saints was first invented by Pope John XV in 995 AD.

Lent and Good Friday began in 988 AD.

The Mass was first declared to be a sacrifice of Christ in 1050 AD.

Celibacy of the priesthood and nuns was first practised in 1079 AD.

The Rosary was introduced by Peter the Hermit in 1090 AD.

Selling Indulgences began in 1190 AD.

The Doctrine of Transubstantiation was adopted in 1215 AD.

Confession of sins to man began in 1215 AD.

Adoration of the wafer was first introduced by Pope Honorius in 1220 AD.

Interpretation of the Bible was forbidden to laity in 1229 AD.

The Scapular was declared a charm against dangers in 1287 AD.

Seven Sacraments were declared in 1439 AD.

Tradition was established as infallible authority in 1545 AD.

The Apocryphal books were added to the Bible in 1546 AD.

The Immaculate Conception of the Virgin Mary was dreamed up in 1546 AD.

Mary was declared to be the Mother of God in 1931 AD.

A whole book could be written on the dogmas which the hierarchy of Rome have added to the doctrine of Christianity as laid out in the Holy Scriptures. Through her pagan dogmas and traditions she is guilty of corrupting God's people, by threatening them with damnation if they fail to comply with her lies, and is a fulfilment of:

*'Even him whose coming is after the working of Satan with all power and signs and lying wonders, and with all deceivableness of unrighteousness in them that perish; because they received not the love of the truth, that they might be saved.*

*And for this cause God shall send them a strong delusion, that they should believe a lie: that they all might be damned who believe not the truth . . .'* (2 Thess 2:9–12)

Oh that God's creation, man, would renounce the teaching of Rome and every other pagan religion and believe the truth, and be saved!

When the truth is constantly rejected, God can lift His grace and leave man to believe that which is false, in order that they may be condemned, because of their refusal to trust and rely on the truth.

The eternal destination of every living soul depends on whether we believe the truth as recorded in the scriptures, or the traditions and dogmas of mere men.

## The Rosary Prayer

Many Roman Catholics have been taught to worship the Blessed Virgin Mary as 'Queen of Heaven' and must celebrate her miraculous bodily ascent into Heaven on August 15th every year. Can the following, which is printed in the Catholic Rosary Book of Prayers by the Rev Daniel A Lord, S.J., be substantiated by the Bible?:

'For a long time Jesus left His Mother on earth. He wanted her to take care of His Apostles and be the Mother of the New Church. Then one day He quietly sent for her, and she died with a smile. The Apostles came from all over the earth to be at her deathbed. They carried her body to the grave and laid it gently in the ground.

Saint Thomas came late, after the burial. When the Apostles took him to the grave they found it empty and open. Where Mary's body had rested, beautiful lilies were growing. Jesus had sent His angels to bring the body of His Mother to Heaven.

It was too pure to rest in the earth. It had served him so well that it must at once enjoy the happiness of Heaven . . .

She had never committed the slightest sin, so in Heaven she was to have her reward.

Body and soul, Mary entered Heaven. Her Son, Jesus, met her and took her in His grateful arms. The Heavenly Father said, 'This is my dear, devoted daughter'.

The Divine Son said, 'This is my dear, faithful Mother'.

The Holy Spirit said, 'This is my sweet, pure bride'.

And the saints and angels called, 'This is our Queen'.

So Jesus, the Kings of Kings, seated her on her throne, on her head He placed a glorious crown of stars. But Mary looked down to see her children on earth, for now she could help her sons and daughters to reach Heaven.

Mary is the Queen of Heaven!

But she is our loving Mother who protects us with her power.'

A very lovely little story, simple enough for a child to understand. The Rosary Prayer Book is beautifully illustrated with 'holy pictures', but is it scriptural? No! It certainly is not. We have yet another example of how Rome deliberately manipulates the truth and turns to lying fables in order to keep her followers in darkness. Whilst claiming adherance to the truth, she violates it with every word.

Mary's death is not recorded in scripture, nor is there any mention of Mary being the Mother of the New Testament Church let alone the 'Mother of God'. Mary was not sinless, neither can she help anyone into Heaven, nor protect anyone by her power. She did not bodily ascend into Heaven, and, last but not least, she is not the 'Queen of Heaven', which is one of the names by which Baal was worshipped in the Old Testament.

According to scripture, the Church has neither a Mother nor a Queen of Heaven, but a Saviour. All who believe the truth shall be saved; all who believe falsehood, shall be damned.

> *'For the husband is the head of the wife, even as Christ is the head of the Church: and He is the Saviour of the body.'* (Eph 5:23)

Jesus, not Mary, said:

> *'I am the way, the truth, and the life: no man cometh unto the Father, but by ME'* (John 14:6)

Was Mary sinless?

> *'For all have sinned, and come short of the glory of God'.* (Romans 3:23)

All includes Mary; and she herself verified that she was a sinner in need of a Saviour:

> *' . . . My soul doth magnify the Lord, and my spirit hath rejoiced in God my Saviour.'* (Luke 1:46–47)

Mary would never have made such a declaration had she been without sin. But being a descendant of

Adam, she thereby acknowledges that she had inherited the stain of original sin with the rest of humanity.

*'By one man (Adam) sin entered the world and death by sin: and so death passed upon all men, for that all have sinned.'* (Romans 5:12)

Although Mary had inherited original sin, being a descendant of Adam, she knew that the baby which would be born of her would be holy and sinless. The baby that was to be conceived in her womb would not be conceived in the normal way, by the seed of man, therefore would not be tainted with original sin, which had passed to all mankind from Adam. Her baby was to be miraculously conceived by the power of the Holy Ghost. The blood of the baby would be holy blood.

The baby would be a boy. His name would be Jesus. He would be the Son of God, the Saviour of the World. (See Luke 1:28–35)

Today, Rome claims that not only Jesus, but Mary also, was miraculously conceived. The dogma of Mary's immaculate conception was first taught and believed in 1854, and cannot be substantiated by the Word of God.

There is not one scripture reference in the whole Bible that can lead anyone to believe that Mary bodily ascended into Heaven. In fact, the scriptures teach the exact opposite. Since the ascension of Jesus:

'. . . *No man* (meaning man or woman) *hath ascended up to heaven* (in bodily form), *but he that came down*

*from heaven, even the son of man which is in heaven.'*
(John 3:13)

Jesus came down from Heaven; the power of the Highest overshadowed Mary; He was immaculately conceived, by the third part of the Godhead, whose veins flowed with Holy Blood.

Although He was the Son of God, He was the Son of Man – in that He was born of a woman, made from man.

*'And the Lord God caused a deep sleep to fall upon Adam, and he slept, and he took one of his ribs and closed up the flesh instead thereof.*

*And the rib which the Lord God had taken from the man, made he a woman . . .'* (Gen 2:21–22)

The dogma of the assumption or rapture of Mary is one of Rome's most recent deceptions, which was neither believed nor taught until 1950–51, and which contradicts the written Word of God.

Another of Rome's heresies is that 'Mary remained a perpetual virgin'. After the Virgin Birth of Jesus, Mary and Joseph had a normal husband and wife relationship and she conceived both sons and daughters by the seed of her husband, Joseph.

*'And Joseph . . . knew her not until she had brought forth her first born son, and he called his name Jesus.'*
(Matt 1:25)

According to Matthew 13:55–56, Mary and Joseph had four sons, named in Scripture as James, Joses, Simon and Judas – and daughters.

# The Wide Road

*'All scripture is given by inspiration of God, and is profitable for doctrine, for reproof, for correction, for instruction in righteousness'.* (2 Tim 3:16)

We can put our full faith, hope and trust in the inspired Word of God, knowing without the slightest shadow of a doubt that the prophets and apostles did not speak of themselves. They delivered unto us that which they received from the Lord.

To acquaint oneself with the ways of God, we must get to know the Holy Scriptures. The Word of God is our spiritual food and we are told:

*'Man cannot live by bread alone but by every word that proceedeth out of the mouth of God'.* (Matt 4:4)

Sadly, most Catholics that I have spoken with confess that they do not regularly read the Bible, nor study the doctrines of their Church. They just accept what they are told without question, and trust in the authority of the Church.

If, during our lifetime here on earth, we just accept what we are told and blindly follow the traditions of our Church, without checking that its dogmas and traditions agree with the inspired Word of God, we could be carried along the wide road that leads to destruction.

Those on that road will one day be resurrected from the dead to stand before the Judgement Throne of God, and whosoever is not found written in the Book of Life will be cast into the Lake of Fire. (See Revelation 20:11–15).

On that dreadful day of judgement, the sinner will try to vindicate himself:

'But Lord, Father Morris said. . .'

Before the sinner can finish the sentence, the Word of God will thunder in his ears:

It is written, call no man father upon the earth, for one is your father, which is in Heaven. (See Matthew 23:9).

'But Lord, Father Mor. . . I mean, my priest told me, if I faithfully prayed the Rosary I would be saved.'

There is Salvation in and through none other than Jesus Christ, there is no other name given among men, whereby you can be saved. (See Acts 4:12).

You rejected the truth and believed a lie.

'But God, I have faithfully confessed my sins to the priest and done penance as directed.'

It is written, one is justified freely by my grace through the redemption that is in Christ Jesus. (See Romans 3:24).

'But God, I have never once failed to attend the sacrifice of the Mass on Sunday, for the last ten years.'

Sanctification came through the offering of the Body of Jesus Christ, once for all. (See Hebrews 10:10).

'But God, I have prayed daily to your Mother and the Saints, and often decorated the Shrines of the Queen of Heaven.'

I am the Everlasting Father, my Divinity has no parentage. There is one mediator between God and men, one mediator of the New Covenant, the man Christ Jesus. (See 1 Tim 2:5; Heb 12:24).

You provoked me to anger with your detestable graven images. (See Jer 8:19).

In a last desperate attempt to save himself from eternal damnation, the sinner cries out:

'Hail Mary, full of grace and pity, help me, help me, help me!'

Not a sound can be heard in the Judgement Hall. Frantically the sinner looks around him; watching, waiting for the appearance of the Blessed Virgin. She would place herself between himself and God, she would obtain pardon for him. The tender, merciful heart of Mary could not reject him in this moment of utter desperation.

Suddenly, but too late, he realises that his Church, his Pope, his Bishops, his Priests have deceived him. Their doctrines, which are the commandments of men, have seduced his heart. Instead of honouring Mary he had been insulting her. She would have no part in the evil traditions of men which had sought to place her in equality with the Godhead.

Mary, the special vessel, chosen by God to give birth to the Saviour of the World, totally submitted her will to the eternal laws of truth, justice and holiness of God, as is expressed in the Bible.

Knowing that there was no second chance, the sinner dejectedly sinks to his knees and confesses 'Jesus Christ is Lord', for every tongue shall confess it (Phil 2:10–11).

The Eternal Father will have the last word:

*'Depart from me, all ye workers of iniquity.'*

(Luke 13:27)

## Another God

*'Beware lest any man spoil you through philosophy and vain deceit, after the traditions of men, after the rudiments of the world, and not after Christ.'* (Col 2:8)

All who pin their faith and hope in deceitful traditions, which are the commandments of mere man, turn away from following Christ. One cannot follow both Christ and man-invented, devil-inspired traditions, because they are in opposition to each other.

Although the Papacy claims adherence to the Holy Trinity, she violates it approximately eight hundred million times, on a daily basis. The Trinity is a union of Three in One, God the Father, God the Son and God the Holy Ghost. In the 1930s, the 'infallible' Pope set himself up as god and turned the Holy Trinity into an Unholy Quartet. Mary was 'deified' and included in the Godhead as the 'Queen of Heaven' and the 'Mother of God'.

Every time Catholics utter the words, 'Hail Mary, Mother of God', they are denying the Holy Trinity. There are approximately eight hundred million people in the world today whose hearts have been seduced by Rome's traditions. If every one of these poor, deluded people says every day: 'Hail Mary, Mother of God, pray for us sinners now, and at the hour of our death', it means that Satan has succeeded in causing God's creation, Man, however unwittingly, to deny the Three in One Holy Trinity, and blaspheme the Godhead 800 million times each day. Rome's claim of adherance to the Holy

Trinity is a lie, a diabolical lie, a great deception, through which she is leading millions into apostasy.

Rome is not a Christian denomination in any true sense. A Christian denomination teaches, preaches and practices that which is recorded in the Bible. She is a counterfeit of the true Church of Christ, an opponent of the Biblical gospel. She misuses the gospel as a great smokescreen to conceal her iniquities, tyrannies, superstitions and idolatries.

Mary never was, is, or ever will be the 'Mother of God'. She was the Mother of Jesus' humanity, but she never was, is, or will be, the Mother of His Divinity. Jesus said:

*'I am Alpha and Omega, the First and the Last.'*
(Revelation 1:11)

If Mary were the Mother of God, it would mean that she existed before God. To exist before God would 'make her God'. Therefore the deception behind the words, 'Hail Mary, Mother of God' exalts Mary to equality with the Godhead. All who pray to the 'Mother of God' are praying to 'another god', 'a false god', the god of this world, Satan himself, who has sought to be worshipped as God since the day in Heaven when he rebelled against the Everlasting Father of the Holy Trinity. The Word of God remains unchanged.

*'Thou shalt have no other gods before me.'* (Exodus 20:3)

Satan has diverted worship from God to Mary, by getting the Papacy, the enemy of the gospel of Jesus Christ, deliberately and skilfully to deceive millions of God's people into honouring another god, a

Mother god, who, through her tender, merciful heart can supposedly save her children from the wrath of an angry God by her intercessions. This diabolical deception will lead its adherents into the Lake of Fire, because there is no salvation in Mary, despite this being claimed.

Rome unashamedly defies God with graven images of the 'Queen of Heaven' and so-called Saints.

> *'Thou shalt not make unto thee any graven image or any likeness of anything that is in heaven above, or that is in the earth beneath, or that is in the water under the earth.'* (Exodus 20:4)

Most Catholics would deny that they worship idols, because the prince of this world (Satan) has blinded their minds. Although unable to see the idolatries committed within their own Church, they are the first to point a finger at the Buddhist, who bows before images of Buddha. The plain fact is, an idol is an idol, whether it be an image of Mary, of Buddha, of a Saint or a Cow.

> *'Thou shalt not bow down thyself to them, nor serve them, for I the Lord thy God am a jealous God, visiting the iniquity of the fathers upon the children unto the third and fourth generations of them that hate me.'* (Exodus 20:5)

God has strictly forbidden His people to make images, to bow before them or to venerate them in any way. As God abhors idolatry, He looks upon idolaters as those who hate Him. The 'act' of kneeling or bowing to an image is an act of worship. Whether it be a statue of Mary, Jesus, a so-called

Saint, a crucifix, the Host, and even a simple, plain cross, if venerated or bowed before, is idolatrous. To present candles, incense or any other object to an idol is sacrificing to 'another god' which thing God hates:

*'Little children, keep yourselves from idols.'* (1 John 5:21)

## The Queen of Heaven

Will you put your faith and hope in Jesus Christ or the Pope?

Will you follow the traditions of men or the Word of God?

Will you trust in the works of your own hands or the blood of the Lamb shed on the cross?

Will you worship the 'Queen of Heaven' or the King of Kings?

Worship of the 'Queen of Heaven' originated from Babylon, and was practised by the Babylonian pagans long before the birth of Christ. Indeed it is mentioned in the Old Testament (Jeremiah 7:18). Semiramis, inspired by Satan, invented a secret, mystery religion, whereby he (Satan) would be worshipped through her, which would rob God of the worship due to Him, from his creation, Man.

Satan set her up as the divine mother, and gave her great, supernatural, satanic power. When Semiramis died, she was given the grand title of 'Queen of Heaven'.

To understand how the worship of the 'Queen of Heaven' spread throughout the nations of the world, we need to go back to Genesis, chapter eleven.

The Babylonian pagans boasted that they would build a tower and its 'top would reach to heaven'. God put an end to their folly, pride and ambition, which was an affront to Him. He confounded their language, so that they could not understand each other's speech and scattered them throughout the world.

God could have consumed these rebels in a moment, but He is a merciful God; He gets no pleasure in any man's destruction. He gave them the chance to repent of their pagan practices, pride and arrogance. Sadly, they paid no attention to God's admonition.

In all the countries where God scattered them, they continued to practice their cult or religion which had been inaugurated and established secretly by Semiramis. They elected a leader and named him 'Supreme Pontiff'; he took charge and led all religious ceremonies. They made images of their beloved Mother goddess with child Tammuz, in her arms, which they bowed down to, adored and venerated as their divine Mother. The people of the countries where the Babylonions had settled became intrigued by this religion and soon were drawn into her web of deception.

New members were baptised into the cult with a baptism of sprinkling with water, and a mark was placed upon them by the Supreme Pontiff.

Worship of the divine mother with child spread throughout the nations of the world. As languages were confounded at Babel, the Queen of Heaven became known by different names.

To the Chinese, she became known as 'Shing-moo' (Holy Mother). the Germans worshipped the Virgin 'Hertha' with child in arms. The Etruscans (an ancient country in central Italy) called her 'Nutria'. The Druids worshipped 'Virgo-Patitura' (Mother of God). In India she became 'Indrant Isi' and child 'Iswara'. To the Greeks she became 'Aphrodite' or 'Ceres'. She became 'Venus' or 'Fortuna' to the Romans and her child became 'Jupiter'. In Asia the mother was known as 'Cybele' and the child as 'Deoius'. (See 'The Two Babylons' by Rev A. Hislop).

Even the Jews, God's chosen people, were seduced by the religion and were guilty of burning incense to the Queen of Heaven and worshipping a counterfeit deity. Time after time, throughout the generations, God sent His prophets to warn the Jews that destruction would overtake them if they continued to worship other gods. They closed their ears to the truth and refused to hear the Word of God. God's anger burned against them and Jerusalem was utterly destroyed.

Jeremiah the prophet was sent to remind them that Jerusalem and Judah had been brought to utter desolation. He reminded the children of Israel of their sins which had provoked God to anger. He reminded them of their wickedness in giving honour and worship to counterfeit deities. He reminded them how the God of Israel had been rejected for imposter gods. He reminded them that they had done abominable things which God hates. Jeremiah warned that further destruction would overtake them if they continued with the pagan practices of their fathers.

They obstinately refused to turn from their idolatries and submit to the Word of God, brought through God's prophet. They defiantly delared to Jeremiah:

> *'We will not listen unto thee, we will do which is forbidden and run the risk of that which is threatened. We will contine to burn incense to the Queen of heaven; our father's priests and kings did it. It was done in Judah and Jerusalem, not only in shady groves but out in the streets; it was the practise of our mother-church. In Jerusalem our Fathers had plenty of everything that was good, they wanted for nothing.'*
>
> (See Jeremiah 44:16–19 (author's paraphrase))

The Jews chose to forget that it was their own wickedness which had ended the prosperity of Jerusalem, and believed what they wanted to believe. They hardened their hearts against the Word of God and refused to hear that the destruction of Israel was a result of their father's worship of the Queen of Heaven, their idolatries, burning incense and sacrifices to other gods.

They twisted the truth and said that the judgements had come because of 'leaving off' the burning of incense to the Queen of Heaven. See Jeremiah 44. Then Jeremiah said:

> *'The incense that ye burned in the cities of Judah and in the streets of Jerusalem, ye and your fathers, your kings and your princes, and the people of the land, did not the*

*Lord remember them, and came it not into his mind so that the Lord could no longer bear, because of the evil of your doings and because of the abominations which ye have committed therefore is your land a desolation, and an astonishment, and a curse, without an inhabitant at this day.*

*Because ye have burned incense and because ye have sinned against the Lord, and not obeyed the voice of the Lord, nor walked in his law, nor his statutes, nor in his testimonies, therefore this evil is happened unto you, as at this day.'* (Jer 44:21–23)

God is merciful and longsuffering, so the evil deeds of their fathers had gone unpunished for a very long time, but God's patience came to an end. He could no longer bear to look upon the abominations that were being committed against Him. The wrath of God was poured out bringing destruction to Judah and Jerusalem and an end to their prosperity.

Still they refused to see it God's way, and put a contrary explanation as to why the judgement had come. They chose to believe the judgement had come as a result of them laying off the burning of incense to the 'Queen of Heaven'.

The women were more guilty of idolatries than were the men. The men were generally atheists and cared for no god, and allowed their wives to defiantly make cakes as a meat offering and give drink as a drink offering to the 'Queen of Heaven'.

Once again, the Word of God came through the prophet, Jeremiah:

*'Thus saith the Lord of hosts, the God of Israel . . . Ye and your wives have both spoken with your mouths, and*

*fulfilled with your hand, saying we will surely perform our vows that we have vowed to burn incense to the queen of heaven and to pour out drink offerings unto her. Ye will surely accomplish your vows and surely performs your vows. Therefore hear ye the Word of the Lord, all Judah that dwell in the land of Egypt; Behold I have sworn by my great name, saith the Lord, that my name shall no more be named in the mouth of any man of Judah in all the land of Egypt saying, The Lord God liveth. Behold I will watch over them for evil, and not for good, and all the men of Judah that are in the land of Egypt shall be consumed by the sword and by famine, until there be an end of them.'* (Jeremiah 44:25–27)

And so it happened as the Lord had spoken! God has used the children of Israel as a testimony and example to every nation and its people, who continue to defy Him by worshipping counterfeit deities, honour the 'Queen of Heaven', burn incense to pagan gods, continue in idolatry and sacrifices to other gods.

God is merciful and longsuffering, but be assured, He will not forever withhold His judgement. Every item of religious regalia, superstition, saint worship, image worship, relic worship, 'Queen of Heaven' worship, within the Roman Catholic religion can be traced back to its origins in the ancient religion of Babylon.

The Church of Rome continues to spread and deceive multitudes with her devil-inspired Babylonian traditions. She impudently defies God by burning incense to the 'Queen of Heaven', angers God by causing His people to worship a counterfeit deity, and rob Him of the honour and worship that is due to the God of Israel Himself.

Will you continue to provoke God to anger by praying to and honouring the 'Queen of Heaven' or 'Mother of God'? If Rome has tricked and deceived you, and caused you to worship and honour the prince of this world, Satan, if she has caused you to commit abominable sins against God, hear the Word of the Lord and 'come out of her' whilst God's grace and mercy prevail.

## *Chapter 6*

# The Great Apostasy

When Rome became a World Empire she assimilated into her system the heathen practices and traditions from the various countries over which she ruled.

During 536 BC Babylon was captured and left in ruins, and the centre of occultism finally came to rest in Rome. It was during the rule of the Roman Empire that God came in the form of the man, Christ Jesus, was crucified, died and rose from the dead. He ascended into Heaven and sent the Holy Spirit to establish the New Testament Church on earth.

The Jewish nation was the first to stubbornly oppose Christianity, but became a relatively unimportant factor when Jerusalem was destroyed by the Romans, approximately fifty years after the establishment of the New Testament Church.

Christianity and pagan Rome clashed immediately, as early Christians refused to compromise or join in any way with heathen beliefs. The Church of Christ had no super-government of any kind, every local congregation was an independant unit, with no-one exercising authority over them. There were two kinds of officers in a congregation – the elder and the deacon. The elders were the superior officers and all elders were on perfect equality. The

Church had no creed apart from truth revealed in the Old Testament, the works of Jesus and the New Testament letters on doctrine.

The mode of worship was very simple, having nothing that would appeal to pride or vainglory. Their praises to the Lord were generally without musical accompaniment. Because of its simplicity and the fact that Christianity was unpopular, they were spared the contaminating influence of those who used the gospel as a means of personal advancement.

As a result of believers refusing to collaborate with Roman paganism, they suffered great persecution. They were falsely accused, tortured and thrown to the lions by the Romans. Christianity soon became widely scattered as believers fled for their lives.

There were no public schools in those days. Few could read or write; there were no printing presses and subsequently few books. As Greek ceased to be the main language, it became increasingly difficult for those who could read to know New Testament teaching.

The mystery of iniquity was already at work and Paul warned Christ's disciples:

> *'For I know this, that after my departure shall grevious wolves enter among you, not sparing the flock.*
>
> *Also, of your own selves shall men arise, speaking perverse things, to draw away disciples after them.'*
>
> (Acts 20:29–30)

They were to watch out for those false brethren, seducers and false teachers, who would enter in amongst them. Even some of the disciples would pervert the truth, in order to draw a following for themselves.

Less than one hundred years after the resurrection of Jesus, the first steps towards apostasy were taken. The seducers and false teachers began to work on those Christians who were lacking in knowledge, and sought a following after themselves. Church Councils were set up to discuss religious matters. Those elders who sought a following for themselves began to meet together from different congregations at some central point. Whatever was decided upon at these Councils or Synods, was bound upon the people when the elders returned to their home congregations. These fame-seeking elders were soon set up as Bishops. They had departed from the divine pattern of elders of equal rank governing each congregation.

The Nicene Creed was formulated in 325 AD by the Council of Nicea. It was a human creed mainly based on the commandments of men. Yet it held to the truth that Jesus Christ was God, made mainfest in the flesh, against the doctrine of Arianism, which held to the teaching that Christ was a created being, therefore inferior to God. An attempt was made to bind all aspects of the creed upon Christians, then force was applied to compel conformity, which resulted in great persecution.

Three great theological schools were set up by the fame-seeking disciples. In each case they had been encouraged by seducers and false teachers. These were Alexandria, under Clement and Origin: Asia

Minor under Irenaeus: Carthage in North Africa under Tertullian and Cyprian.

Through ambition and pride they had been seduced by false teachers. They each held to different ideas and doctrines which conformed to human needs rather than New Testament teaching. And so it was as Paul had prophesied:

> *'Also of your ownselves shall men arise, speaking perverse things to draw away disciples unto them'* (Acts 20:30)

By the end of the third century the doctrine of 'infant baptism' was believed by the majority. Remember, admission into Babylon's ancient cult was by mode of a baptism of 'sprinkling of water', and marked by the initiating priest. Babylon's ceremony of initiation into her mystery cult was remodelled into 'infant baptism', sprinkling with water, and the mark was replaced with the sign of the Latin cross on the infant's forehead by the Bishop.

Babylon's initiation rite is practised faithfully by both Anglicans and Roman Catholics even to this day. The New Testament doctrine of believers' baptism (full immersion) to follow repentance, became the exception. Finally, after many centuries, it became practically obsolete, as did the fruit and gifts of the Holy Spirit, even though some groups of believers did still experience them.

Constantine became Emperor of Rome early in the fourth century, by which time 'paganised christianity' was rapidly gaining popularity. Before the first coming of the Lord Jesus Christ, the Roman Empire was spiritually united by Babylon's ancient cult. Everyone adhered to it one way or another, except perhaps a minority of Jews, who had remained faithful to the Old Covenant. Therefore Rome, as a World Empire, enjoyed both religious and political unity.

Constantine was far-seeing enough to realise that religious disunity could cause political unrest. Unity was of utmost importance. He was concerned that this new religion which was gaining popularity at an alarming rate would cause political division. So he himself 'professed' conversion, though in reality he never was a born-again believer. His first step after his claimed conversion was to order all persecution against the Church to cease.

In order that he might have a measuring stick he adopted and altered the Nicene Creed. This creed, we must remember, was a human creed, with a smattering of the truth. When the creed was written a new religion was born requiring a new designating term, which is the origin of the name 'Catholic'. There were then two distinct bodies; those who subscribed to the new creed, designating themselves by the new name 'Catholic', and on the other side there were those who were content with the Scriptures as their creed and with the name it authorised.

The word 'Catholic' is a Greek word, meaning 'universal'. There never was a time when there were not some dissenters, as all men did not believe as the Catholics did, therefore the party calling itself 'Catholic' was never universal. When they divided into 'Greek Catholics' and 'Roman Catholics' its claim of being universal was even more ridiculous (for further information see 'Catholicism against Itself' by O.C. Lambert).

The purpose of human creeds is to try to force unity by compelling the minority to conform. Unity through a state religion is a valuable political asset. Constantine became the High Priest of the New Church and Defender of the Catholic faith.

Those who failed to comply with the new state religion were persecuted and driven out of their temples. The temples were decorated with beautiful images of Semiramis, the Babylonian 'Queen of Heaven', with child Tammuz in her arms. Did the new Church, which 'professed' Christianity destroy the pagan images of the mother goddess? Sadly, no! They simply changed the idol's name to Mary, 'Mother of Jesus' and looked upon them as 'Mary with Child Jesus' in her arms. The Church of Rome did not give Mary Semiramis's full title as Mother of God until fifty seven years ago, when the Pope of that day declared her to be 'Mother of God'.

So the worship of the pagan goddess, Semiramis, was transferred to Mary. When it became obvious to Constantine's subjects that the Catholic Church would allow them to continue worshipping their beloved 'Queen of Heaven' under a different name, millions professed conversion to the New Church.

The Emperor had achieved the religious and political unity that was necessary to further his goals of ambition, and he conquered the whole of Europe. Prior to the decisive battle outside Rome, Constantine is said to have seen a vision of a cross of light in the evening sky and beneath it the words, 'In this sign, conquer!'. A further vision told him to set the sign of Christ on his own helmet and on the shields of his men. This he did, and went forth to plunder, murder and conquer, claiming to do his dirty deeds in the name of Christ. Plunder and murder are not the Lord's means of conquering men's hearts. Jesus told his disciples:

> *'Go into all the world and preach the gospel to every creature. He that believeth and is baptised shall be saved; but he that believeth not, shall be damned.'*
>
> (Mark 16:15–16)

The Emperor's means of turning the people of the nations to Catholicism, through plunder and war, was not the means through which God commanded His disciples to conquer men's hearts. Constantine either lied about the visions, or they were satanic apparitions of an ankh cross, an Egyptian occult cross, as are the appartitions of the so called 'Queen of Heaven' today.

As the years passed slowly but surely, more and more rites and rituals of Babylon's ancient religion were introduced into the Catholic Church. The hierarchy took full advantage of the fact that few people could either read or write. So the trusting public were easily deceived. Those who could read, who had some knowledge of the scriptures, naturally objected, on the grounds that such practices were not scriptural.

The hierarchy soon overcame all objections. They simply forged a document and added the name of an apostle. The forgery would then be 'discovered' and used as proof that the new practice was, after all, scriptural. This turned out to be a most effective method of introducing new dogmas, and its use became widespread during the Middle Ages.

The most outstanding thing in Church History is the great apostasy. It continued to increase through the generations. Rome fought battle after battle and forced the people of the nations with which she came into contact to convert to Catholicism or die. She continued to add new dogmas as she saw fit. The hierarchy willingly turned out forgeries with relatively clear consciences because of the dogma of 'mental reservation', which is a general law permitting Catholics to lie. A lie could be told provided it furthered Rome's aspirations; with them, such lying is not sinful.

History tells the story of the Bartholomew massacre. Rome sought to rid France of Bible-believing Christians. On August 22nd, 1572 at twelve o'clock midnight, the Pope's soldiers attacked. Within three days, literally thousands of believers were massacred. The bodies were thrown into the river and the blood ran through the streets until it met the river. Thus the river took on the appearance of a river of blood. In their fury, they even slew their own; if they had the slightest suspicion that a soldier was losing his faith in the Pope, he too was murdered. So much for unity with the Protestant Church.

In Ireland during 1641, the Pope planned a general uprising for the whole country. All Bible-believing Christians were to be killed. No mercy was to be shown, even the children, elderly and invalids were murdered; massacred by their neighbours, friends and even relations. For the women, death was the least they had to fear. They were tied to posts, stripped to the waist and their breasts were cut off with shears and they were left to bleed to death. Pregnant women were tied to trees, their bellies were split open, their unborn babies cut out and thrown to the dogs, while the fathers were made to look on. (For further information see Foxe's Book of Martyrs)

## The Need to Expose Rome's Global Strategy

Rome has always sought to use key political leaders as a way of attaining Catholic goals. Hitler, Mussolini and Franco were all defenders of the Roman Catholic Faith and therefore enjoyed full support. They were assisted and financed by the Vatican to conquer the world, believing that this would establish a global Catholic kingdom for Rome, the 1,000 year Reich or Kingdom.

Hitler, a Roman Catholic Nazi, was working in liaison with the Vatican in giving the command which resulted in the death of 6 million Jews and 2½ million Christians. This is documented in 'The Secret History of the Jesuits' by Edmond Paris (p123–138, p172–174)[1] and can be substantiated, despite considerable attempts to suppress the information in the atmosphere of a changed post-war world. However hard it is to accept, the conspiracy we are dealing with is 'principalities and powers' working together to achieve mutual objectives. The end goal justifies whatever means were necessary, and while the current means have changed very considerably the end goal of winning the world for Catholicism still stands. Those who work for this cause are held in honour.

The write-up in the Spanish press on 3rd May, 1946, the day of Hitler's death, read as follows:

> 'Adolf Hitler, son of the Catholic Church, died while defending Christianity . . . Over his mortal remains stands his victorious moral figure. With the palm of the martyr, God gives Hitler laurels of Victory.'
>
> (For further information see 'Smokescreens' by Chick Publications)

We live in a different post-war, 'let's forget the past' world. Is it then necessary to recall the tragedies of the past or bring to light Rome's dark deeds? Three hundred years of civil and spiritual liberty, neglect of the prophetic Word of God and lessons of history are sad marks of the ecumenical days in which we now live. Our nation has become over-confident and underestimated the powers and influence of Rome's intentions to establish a one world church.

Britain's honourable distinction of being the leading witness among the nations for the Gospel of Jesus Christ, and against the errors of Roman Catholicism, are lightly esteemed in our generation. Until shortly before the writing of this book, I knew

During Rome's 'Golden Age', political and religious liberty almost totally disappeared. Free thought, free speech and free worship brought persecution and death. Rome resisted every effort towards civil and religious liberty. Spiritual darkness was the order of Rome's 'Golden Age'. Whilst Rome ruled, the Bible remained a closed book. Spiritual darkness covered the earth and gross darkness the people.

## The Reformation

> *'And I saw one of his heads as it were wounded to death . . .'* (Rev 13:3)

The Reformation struck a great blow to the root of pagan Roman Catholicism. As the Holy Scriptures were not translated into English until 1380–82 the Church of England was a Church without a Bible. The religion of our British fathers was a religion without knowledge, faith, justification, regeneration or sanctification, a religion without any clear view of Jesus or the Holy Ghost except in rare instances.

The Church of England was simply a religion of Mary worship, Saint worship, image worship, relic worship, pilgrimages and processions, penance, absolution, Masses, almsgiving and blind obedience to the priest. The priests took the people's money and undertook to secure their salvation. Britain desperately needed the light of the Gospel to dispel the darkness.

Between 1380–82 John Wycliffe diligently set about the task of translating the New Testament into English. His friend, Nicholas Hereford, undertook the translation of the Old Testament. Once the work of translating the Bible into a language that could be understood by the people was completed, they were then faced with the tremendous task of 'copying' the new translation for distribution amongst the people. As the printing press had not yet been invented, 'every word' from Genesis to Revelation had to be written with great care and diligence.

Wycliffe realised that the only remedy for Britain was the Word of God. Our land at that time had just been ravished with the awful 'black death' plague, through which half the population had died. Besides plague and disease there were agricultural disputes and perpetual battles. The Bible was a forbidden book. According to the Papacy it was 'dangerous to the unlearned'. Regardless of Rome's threats concerning the Bible, Wycliffe and his co-workers in Christ pressed on with the task of making the Bible available in English to the people of Britain.

The fourteenth century attempt to 'Reform Britain' through the introduction of the Bible was ruthlessly opposed by Rome. Yet Rome was no match for the written Word of God, for the Bible was not abolished but merely 'driven underground'. Wycliffe's Bibles were read in secret, and one hundred and seventy copies have survived the persecutions of men and the passing of time, to this day.

What a tremendous example, labour of love, patient endurance and bravery was shown by these saints of God, who have the honour of being the first to make the Bible available in English to the people of Britain.

Fear being Rome's method of keeping her people under subjection, she passed a law in the year 1408 which forbade any translations of scripture into English. All persons were warned against reading such a book, under the dread penalty of excommunication. With the invention of the printing press approximately one hundred and fifty years later, those days of gross darkness and oppression began to break, and a new day for Britain was dawning.

The English language had changed a lot with the passing of a century and a half, and technology had advanced to the invention of the printing press. It was then possible for the Bible to be printed in the more modern English language. William Tyndale was God's chosen man. He was a man with a heart after God, who fearlessly preached the truth and publicly exposed Rome's heresies, without counting the cost to self. Of course, he was arrested and charged with 'preaching heresies' in and about the town of Bristol. He got off lightly with only a warning never to preach again. His main ambition was to translate the Bible from Greek into the new modern English language, in order that the ordinary man in the street would have the opportunity to read the Bible for himself.

Tyndale had been working on the translation of the Bible for approximately six months when the enemy struck. His friends, in whose home he lodged, became fearful. If it came to light that he was translating the forbidden book in their home, they would be arrested for aiding a heretic, so he had to move. England could not offer him a place to continue his work, he was forced to leave his own beloved country and sail to Hamburg. From there he was forced to move on to Cologne, where he finally finished the translation of the New Testament. It was necessary to employ two printers to help him set up the type, and all went well until one evening when his printer employees were conversing about their work in a local tavern. Their conversation was overheard and Tyndale's project was ruined. He barely had time to collect his precious printed papers and depart, as the hounds of the Papacy were on his tracks.

The desire to see his beloved England throw off the shackles of Rome drove him on. His next destination was Worms, and there his first edition of the New Testament was finally completed. The spies had been at work for some time. London and the East Coast ports at Yarmouth, Kings Lynn and Hull were all on the alert and watching out for the coming of the objectionable book. In spite of Rome's efforts to keep the Bible a closed book in Britain, the Bibles were well disguised and safely transported from Continental ports to England. The 'smugglers' had wonderful success and half of Britain's population was eager to read the forbidden book.

Tyndale needed money to pay off his debts and the Lord arranged a curious set of circumstances. A number of the Bibles were sold to the Bishop of London, who arranged a public burning of them on 11th February, 1526. This public burning of the New Testament was attended by Cardinal Wolsey, thirty six bishops, abbots and friars. Bishop John Fisher, who had recently been 'canonised' by the Pope, preached on the occasion, and fully approved the 'burning' of the Word of God. The charge against Tyndale was that his work was 'inaccurate'. Time has proved that such a charge was completely absurd. It is yet another testimony and example of how 'the Church – paganised Christianity', was totally hostile to the publication of the Holy Scriptures before the Reformation.

The Lord, in His great wisdom, brought good out of that bad situation. Tyndale's debts were paid off and he was able to start the printing of his second edition, there was a great hue and cry about the burning of God's Word, and last but not least, a percentage of the Bibles escaped the 'great burning ceremony'.

The Spirit of God moved in the hearts of His people and in spite of the risk involved, young men set about the task of selling and distributing the new English Bible throughout England. One of their number was a young lad named Garret, who had successfully sold a number of Bibles in Oxford, then moved on to Bristol, still selling his precious wares. He was fully aware of the dangers involved. If he were caught it would mean vile imprisonment and cruel death. The hounds of the Papacy were waiting for him when he arrived at Bristol. He was imprisoned and eventually put to death. His 'only' crime was distributing the forbidden book. The biggest majority of his co-workers in Christ met with a similar fate, while others suffered terrible public floggings and imprisonment. For them, to live was Christ but to die was gain.

The Papist spies were constantly trying to hunt out Tyndale and he was finally arrested in May, 1535. For fifteen months he endured the terrible trial of imprisonment. Prison cells in those days were damp, dark, windowless dungeons. William Tyndale, a true saint of God, went to be 'with Christ' on 16th October 1536. He was taken from prison, tied to a stake and strangled, after which his body was burnt to ashes. His last prayer was:

'Lord, open the King of England's eyes'.

The answer came with little delay, for within a year his English translation of the Bible received Royal recognition. By the end of 1538, every Parish Church in our land was supplied with its own copy of the English Bible (see 'Heroes of the Reformation' P.T.S. 184 Fleet St, London).

Tyndale did not have the joy of actually seeing his beloved homeland set free from the shackles of Rome, yet through his life's work here on earth, God struck a great blow to the root of pagan Roman Catholicism. Nothing alarmed or outraged the 'priesthood' so much as the spread of the English Bible. For spread it did, not only throughout Britain but throughout the nations of the world.

With a Bible in every Parish Church it became obvious to all who read it that the religion of the priests had no basis in the Holy Scriptures. The Bible was an open book, God's own Word was read round the firesides of the people and the Holy Ghost did His work. The ordinary folk in the street saw for themselves that all things needful to salvation, faith and practise were found within the written Word of God. Their eyes were opened and they saw how Rome had robbed, tricked and deceived them and they turned from the doctrines of demons to the doctrines of Christ. They received the truth with much affliction, but in the joy of the Holy Ghost.

In all situations and circumstances of life we find there are always those who are ready to 'take advantage' of whatever situation. This of course also happened during the days of the Reformation. There were those who plundered Abbey lands and did things which ought never to have been done, being motivated by greed and finacial gain. Henry VIII was by no means a Godly man, neither were the majority of his statesmen, yet the Bible reveals how God used Cyrus and Nebuchadnezzar, regardless of their imperfections, to bring about His will. And so it was with King Henry VIII and his statesmen, God used them to bring about His will. For it certainly was His will that the light of the Gospel of Jesus Christ be shed abroad in the hearts of men.

We must never forget the past, but remember with much gratitude those who protested against the errors of Rome and laid down their lives to bring civil and spiritual liberty to our land. With great thankfulness of heart let us remember the overall results of the Reformation. It brought an

English Bible to our land and the liberty for every man, woman and child to read it! The Reformation opened the door to the Throne of Grace and peace with God for all who sought it! The Reformation delivered Britain from gross darkness and religious deception! The Reformation caused the Church of England to become Protestant, and established reformed Churches in separation from the Church of Rome.

If not for our sake, but the sake of our children and grandchildren, let us:

> '*Stand fast therefore in the liberty wherewith Christ hath made us free and be not entangled again with the yoke of bondage*' (Gal 5:1)

## The Golden Age of Ecumenism

Rome has a global strategy to win the whole world for Catholicism, under the Pope as its true head. If conquest will not work then negotiation and merger are alternative strategies. History has been a mixture of both. As mentioned earlier Jesuit priests actively supported Hitler in his desire to set up the 1,000 year Reich or Kingdom. He was a Catholic and it would be a Catholic kingdom, hence their support. The Nazi Party was 'Catholic Action' in which the Jesuit priests were involved, particularly the Gestapo behind the scenes. The Vatican provided money because of their self-interest to see a Catholic Millenium established. However far-fetched this may seem 50 years on, the world is now a very different place, and in those days of European dictators the Vatican provided very active political and financial support, believing that they would be successful on Rome's behalf, too. After World War Two the climate of opinion changed dramatically, so the Vatican disassociated itself from a defeated Hitler and Mussolini and concentrated on diverting attention onto a new threat – Communism. This was a common enemy for both Catholics and Protestants to unite against, yet even here Rome was involved with the Communist Party in many countries and had considerable influence there, effecting a great deal of control. Nevertheless it became strategically important to denounce Communism as an enemy at that time to focus attention away from the past. This is again documented in 'The Secret History of the Jesuits'.[1]

After the war Fulton J. Sheen launched an anti-communist attack, and the attention of Protestants was shifted from the Vatican to Communism. Rome was busy on many fronts. She infiltrated Jesuit priests into Protestant denominations who frowned on and discouraged anti-Catholic sermons. Hollywood furnished us with exciting films which glorified the Catholic faith. The Second Vatican Council came into existence and we saw how Rome started to change her tactics. Protestants were no longer called heretics but 'separated brethren'. Rome now loved the 'separated brethren'. Suddenly, and remarkably, everything began to change. At the beginning of the 1960's a new warmth and co-operation flowed forth from Rome, the doors to 'unity' were flung open. The twentieth century is to be Rome's 'Golden Age' of peace and unity.

Once again, we see history repeating itself. The Lord Jesus' first coming had caused division within the Roman Empire. With the spread of Christianity, Constantine was losing both political and spiritual power over the people. First he tried putting an end to the division among his subjects by putting Christians to death and feeding them to the lions. The persecution did not have the effect that Constantine hoped for, it only strengthened the Christians' resolve. So he had to change his tactics. He professed 'conversion' to Christianity and used subtle methods of infiltration which produced pagan Roman Catholicism.

Babylon's ancient occult religion had its temples, altars, pictures and images. So has Roman Catholicism today.

Babylon's ancient occult religion had its use of 'holy wafers' and its burning of incense. So does Roman Catholicism today.

Babylon's ancient occult religion had its priests who were presided over by a sovereign pontiff. So has Roman Catholicism today.

Babylon's ancient occult religion had its adoration of a visible representative of the deity. So has Roman Catholicism today.

Babylon's ancient occult religion had its ceremonies of kissing the hand and feet of the infallible sovereign pontiff. So does Roman Catholicism today.

Babylon's ancient occult religion had its stately robes and crowns. So does Roman Catholicism today.

Babylon's ancient occult religion had its adoration of idols and worship of the 'Queen of Heaven'. So does Roman Catholicism today.

Babylon's ancient occult religion had its rural shrines, processions, pretended miracles; its speaking images, weeping images, and bleeding images. So does Roman Catholicism today.

Babylon's ancient occult religion had its canonization of Saints as in the deification of the dead Caesars. So does Roman Catholicism today.

Babylon's ancient occult religion had its enforced celibacy. So does Roman Catholicism today.

Babylon's ancient occult religion had its cruel persecution of those who opposed idolatry. So has Roman Catholicism today, although we don't see it in Britain, yet.

Babylon's ancient occult religion was satanically inspired. So is Roman Catholicism today. The essence of counterfeit religion is to make it look superficially close to the real thing to cause confusion and deception.

Satan revised Babylon's ancient occult religion with the worship of mother and child, and named it Roman Catholicism, simply substituting Mary and Jesus as the 'Madonna and Child'.

Once Roman Catholicism was established Rome returned to her murders and massacres; her ultimate aim being political and religious unity with the Pope as the ruler of the world. The present day

Pope is once again using Constantine's strategy. He professes to being a 'born again, spirit-filled Christian', who speaks in tongues. Slowly, but surely, his subtle methods of infiltration are drawing Christendom into Rome's web. Once the infiltration has achieved its goals, we will once again see Rome's true colours. Mark these words!

Rome's motto is 'semper idem', always the same. There can be no change in any dogma or basic teaching of the Catholic Church, for such a change would be a denial that the Church is the true Church founded by Christ.

The Charismatic movement, which started in the 1950's, was sweeping across the Christian world and was seen as capable of transforming the Church. Rome once again found itself in the same position as in Constantine's day, when the New Testament Church was daily drawing people away from Babylon's occult religion into Christianity. Let us take a look at how Rome re-enacted Constantine's subtle methods of infiltration:

> '*. . . and his deadly wound was healed: and all the world wondered after the beast*' (Rev 13:3)
>
> '*And I beheld another beast coming up out of the earth; and he had two horns like a lamb, and he spake as a dragon. And he exerciseth all the power of the first beast before him, and causeth the earth and them which dwell therein to worship the first beast, whose deadly wound was healed.*' (Rev 13:11–12)

The first beast was 'Pagan Rome', which received a deadly wound and ceased to rule the world.

The second beast is Papal Rome, which will exercise all the power of the first beast before him –

rule the world, and cause the earth and them which dwell therein to worship the first beast, whose deadly wound was healed.

Dialogue began behind the scenes between the then Archbishop of Canterbury, Geoffrey Fisher and the Pope. The outcome was the Pope's first visit to Britain in 1986. He arrived to kiss the ground and claim it for Rome. The five days of the Papal visit to this country must be regarded as five days of shame. Since the Reformation, our nation has known and experienced God's blessing. The Bible made Britain a great nation, now she is in disgrace and is beginning to experience the wrath of Almighty God.

The Archbishop of Arundel said of the Pope's visit to Britain:

'. . . It seems to me that the Pope's presence in our midst for those memorable days has given the Catholic Church a much greater confidence and courage to be what it is . . .

We have a mission, as the Church of Jesus Christ, to the people of this country, and that mission is fulfilled by our own prayer . . . The Holy Father came to confirm our faith . . . he came to give us all a renewed sense of God's call to play a full and active part in the life of the Church.'

The Arundel and Brighton News also reported what the laity thought of the Pope's visit:

'We showed this country that the Catholic Church is alive again, really alive.'

The Church of Rome has always sought the reconversion of the people of Britain to Catholicism. The Pope claims that he and his church are in the direct line of Apostolic succession, and that they are the only repository of spiritual truth. Outside them there is neither truth nor salvation. During his visit to our land, he laid 'claim' to England as his predecessors have, as 'Mary's Dowry'. Of Scotland he said, 'She is a special daughter of the Church of Rome'. The Church of Rome has never relinquished its claim on Britain.

During the afternoon of his first day in England, the Pope went to Buckingham palace and met with Her Majesty the Queen – defender of the Protestant faith. Because of who she is and what she represents, she was attired in black and wore a veil in the presence of the Holy Father of light and truth! The main purpose of the Pope's visit to our shores was to give the Ecumencial Movement a boost. He was lauded by the press and media as 'a great man of peace'. The infiltration, as in Constantine's day, was well and truly under way.

Rome has always been very concerned about the evangelical church and Protestant believers. If they couldn't be eliminated by force as in the past some other method was needed to get them into the Catholic fold, and prevent Catholics from leaving. So they were called 'The Separated Brethren' to be wooed back in.

The main push behind the strategy was to woo well-known evangelical Protestants with a good reputation and high profile and encourage them to show Catholicism in a good light – just another denomination but basically 'one of us' with whom we should have fellowship and seek common ground.

The best known target, highly respected and successful in evangelism, was Billy Graham. If he would endorse Catholicism in a spirit of unity then he could be used to bring Catholics and Protestants together. He has been used to further Rome's ecumenical aims. Having started as a sincere fundamentalist Bible believer, Rome's influence caused him not to preach that Catholics should come out and be separate, rather to stay in.

Because the separation has successfully been blurred, Rome is now presented as an ally in world evangelism; but the real push is for a united church under Rome. Spiritual deception is described in the Bible like drunkenness. You lose your ability to reason and come under an outside influence. This has tragically happened with a number of evangelical leaders, not just Billy Graham, who is perhaps the best known and most widely reported.

C.E. Allen O.S.B., Executive Vice President of Belmont Abbey, North Carolina, wrote of Billy Graham:

> 'I am the one who, being acquainted with Billy Graham, invited him to speak to the Fathers and Nuns, students and guests . . . I have followed Billy Graham's career and I must emphasize that he has been more Catholic than otherwise, and I say that not in a partisan manner but as a matter of fact. Knowing the tremendous influence of Billy Graham among

Protestants and, now, the realization and acknowledgement among Catholics of his devout and sincere appeal to the teaching of Christ, which he alone preaches, I would state that he could bring Catholics and Protestants together in a healthy ecumenic spirit.' (see Smoke Screen, Chick Publications for further information)

Under Rome's influence Billy changed his position from fundamentalist to ecumenist. By 1967, Billy was well and truly under Rome's influence. He received an Honorary Degree of Doctor of Humane Letters from the Roman Catholic College, Belmont Abbey. Five years later, he received the International Franciscan Award in Minneapolis for true ecumenism.

All who 'received' Christ at the Billy Graham crusades were told to 'go back to their original churches'. In this way, the Pope was safeguarding his followers from being drawn into Protestantism. New converts who did not belong to any denomination were divided out amongst the various denominations, including, of course, the Church of Rome. The great prize for Rome was that the world was made to believe that Rome had changed and was eager for her people to respond to the gospel of Christ.

On 13th January 1981 the Pope spent two hours with Dr. Graham, the world's best known Protestant evangelist. The outcome of their meeting was that all enquiries were given to priests and nuns. Billy finally introduced Pope John Paul II as the greatest moral leader of the world.

Rome used Billy, a disciple of Christ, to draw disciples for herself. As there were those within the early Church who fell prey to Rome's subtle means of infiltration and drew away disciples after them, so it still goes on today. Let us heed Paul's warning:

*'Also of your own selves shall men arise, speaking perverse things, to draw away disciples after them'*. (Acts 20:30)

Doctor Billy Graham, who was loved, honoured and respected by the Protestants, gave the Pope a cloak of respectability. They heard his endorsement and, trusting Billy, they gave their love and respect to the one who claims to be the representative of Christ on this earth.

Last, but not least, the Pope had gained respectability in Protestant circles; the world was made to believe that at last Rome was changing and responding to the Gospel of Christ, which enabled Catholics and Protestants to meet together in a spirit of unity. As in Constantine's day, people 'professed' conversion to Christianity, but continued to hold to the entire doctrine of Babylon's occult religion.

God can use any situation and turn it around and use it for His glory, and there were many, and only God knows the number, who came into a living relationship with Christ as a result of the Billy Graham Crusades. Let us take a look at the overall results of the Billy Graham Crusades.

There were those who responded to Billy's call of Salvation, whom God led into His Church, where they sat under the Word of God and came to realise what repentance and deliverance was all about, who grew in the knowledge of God and went on to bear fruit for Him.

The Catholics were made to believe they were 'born again' because they had had an emotional experience. They had responded to the 'soft' gospel message which had not exposed pagan concepts or heretical doctrines, therefore there was no true repentance, no real response and no spiritual rebirth.

## Paganised Charismatic Christianity

The current strategy is to be united in everything possible where Protestants are – missions, local and national, conferences, everything – to show that there really is no difference, no more than say between Anglicans, Methodists and Baptists.

In the early 1950's the Charismatic Movement was sweeping across the Christian world. Rome felt threatened and feared that this move of the Holy Spirit would cause both spiritual and political division in her ranks. The Papacy saw the problem and the opportunity, so the Charismatic Renewal Movement was officially adopted by the Church of Rome and became the Ecumencial Charismatic Renewal Movement. Cardinal Suenens was put in charge of the movement in the Vatican, and the movement enjoyed the active support of Cardinal Bea, Pope Paul II and their successors. Rome's next phase was to promote 'paganised Charismatic Christianity.'

Rome needed to be part of any organisation that was well respected in Protestant circles, any non-denominational organisations which opened their doors to all. The Full Gospel Businessman's Fellowship International had started and was growing rapidly and through this organisation Rome saw a means of breaking down denominational barriers in the cause of unity. Did Jesuit Priests, being the greatest infiltrators the world has ever known, go to work in FGBMFI circles, using the same tactics with which they have successfully infiltrated main line Protestant denominations?

Would the 'separated brethren' accept Roman Catholics as brethren in Christ if they 'spoke in tongues'? Time would tell! If the 'separated brethren' fell into the trap, the spiritual and political unity that was needed to set the Pope up as the spiritual leader of the world could then be realised. If it appeared that God were blessing Catholics, that surely endorsed their doctrine, so a major obstacle to unity could be removed.

Once again Rome was careful to ensure that her followers did not get drawn into any of the Bible preaching Protestant denominations. The FGBMFI is an 'arm' of the Church, which encourages new converts back into their various denominations. Sadly, the organisation makes no distinction between the Protestant denominations whose doctrines are basically grounded in the Word of God and the heretical doctrines and satanic practices of Romanism. Therefore it can be concluded that the organisation of the FGBMFI accepts and respects the Roman Catholic Church as a Christian denomination.

Time has revealed that the 'separated brethren' have fallen – hook, line and sinker – into Rome's ecumenical trap. A remarkable change has taken place; almost the entire Protestant wing of Christianity is on its way right back into the arms of Romanism.

Practising Roman Catholics and Christians fellowship together as 'one' overlooking all doctrinal differences. Preachers who once stood in their pulpits and warned against the rise of the end time apostate world church are today, without realising it, themselves helping to build it up.

In the FGBMFI 'Extra Good News' bulletin report, at Costa Mesa headquarters, March 28th, 1987, Demos Shakarian (founder) wrote:

> 'In the 1952 vision, which was the birth of Full Gospel Businessmen's Fellowship International, not only did I see men everywhere down hearted, depressed and defeated the first time around the world, but the second time God took me in the Spirit around the world. I saw the happiest people on earth praising God with their hands lifted up to Him. In later revelations, the Lord showed me that these men, in their daily lives, would be doing miracles, like those done by the disciples of the early church, and even greater ones.
>
> As He raised up the Full Gospel Businessmen around the world, I saw this mighty move of God grow into an organisation covering 93 nations, nearly 4,000 chapters, and a hundred thousand members strong. I have seen great moves of the Spirit of God which has affected the lives of millions. It was a simple work of God through the Full Gospel Businessmen's Fellowship that can be traced back to the present.

"SEVENTY MILLION CHARISMATIC CATHOLICS" . . . Our greatest fruit in these meetings has been the hundreds and thousands who have received the BAPTISM WITH THE HOLY SPIRIT and healing as well as multitudes receiving salvation . . .'

Rome's trap, to unite Christianity and Catholicism using practising Roman Catholics who speak in tongues, has proved most successful. The question needs to be asked, 'are the tongues spoken by practising Roman Catholics truly the tongues of the Holy Spirit, or are they counterfeit tongues?'

The answer is, as always, found in the Word of God.

*'whosoever transgresseth, and abideth not in the doctrine of Christ, HATH NOT GOD . . .'* (2 John 9)

Practising Roman Catholics do not abide in the doctrine of Christ, therefore they hath not God, and cannot be speaking with the tongues of the Holy Spirit. Only if a person abides in the doctrine of Christ can one speak with the tongues of God's Spirit.

Do we accept African witch doctors as brethren in Christ just because they speak in tongues? Or those who hold to the doctrine of the Mormon religion, as brethren in Christ, just because they speak in tongues? The answer is surely no! Yet many within the Body of Christ accept those who hold to the unbiblical doctrines and satanic practises of Romanism as brethren in Christ, simply because they speak in tongues.

Through ecumenical non-denominational organisations who work for unity and overlook doctrinal differences, Rome has successfully produced pagan Charismatic Christianity.

## Falling Away First

It is a cruel deception to teach that one can be 'born again' and receive the 'gifts of the Holy Spirit' apart from the preaching of repentance and faith, the understanding and the acceptance by faith of the message of the Word of God, the Bible. Having shared my testimony at many chapter dinners of the FGBMFI throughout Britain, I myself have been guilty of this very act, of which I trust God has forgiven me as a result of my repentance and returning to the preaching of His Word. No-one can actually become 'born again' by hearing a testimony alone or through the words of mere men and women. According to the Word of God one is:

> *'Born again, not of corruptible seed, but of incorruptible, BY THE WORD OF GOD'*. (1 Peter 1:23)

Paul said to the Philippian jailer:

> *'Believe on the Lord Jesus Christ and thou shalt be saved, and thy house.'* (Acts 16:31)

Paul's words were not some magic formula for salvation, but were an introduction to a long, Bible based sermon on the subject:

> *'And they spake unto him the Word of the Lord and to all that were in his house.'* (Acts 16:32)

The jailer and his house became 'born again' through believing the 'Word of God' which had been preached to them:

*'Verily verily I say unto you, he that HEARETH MY WORD and believeth on him that sent me hath everlasting life and shall not come into condemnation, but is passed from death unto life'* (John 5:24)

There can be no salvation apart from hearing and believing the incorruptible Word of God. The next step is receiving:

*' . . . as many as received him, to them gave he power to become the sons of God, even to them that believe on his name'* (John 1:12)

Where did their faith to receive Him come from?

*'Faith cometh by hearing and hearing BY THE WORD OF GOD'* (Rom 10:17)

The ministry of the FGBMFI to reach businessmen is an admirable one. However, the policy of not preaching the gospel, but testimony only, denies the convicting power of the Holy Spirit to convict of sin, leading the sinner to repentance and faith. We must do God's work God's way, and not weaken or compromise the message.

Any person or organisation that substitutes the Word of God and the Gospel of Christ with any other means of bringing others to salvation, has 'fallen away' from serving Christ by preaching 'another gospel'. Did Jesus say 'go into all the world and share your personal testimony, and they that believe your testimony shall be saved'? No, he did not! It sounds ridiculous when you think about it. Jesus said:

> *'Go ye into all the world and PREACH THE GOSPEL to every creature. He that believeth and is baptised shall be saved; but he that believeth not shall be damned.*
>
> *And these signs shall follow them that believe; in my name shall they cast out devils, they shall speak with new tongues; they shall take up serpents; and if they drink any deadly thing it shall not hurt them; they shall lay hands on the sick, and they shall recover'* (Mark 16:15–18)

Believers are to 'preach the gospel', for salvation only comes through the hearing and believing of the incorruptible Word of God. After the hearer has heard, believed and received the Holy Spirit by faith, it is the preacher's responsibility to see that the new convert goes through the waters of baptism (full immersion) in obedience to the Lord's commandment:

> *'He that believeth and is baptised shall be saved'* (Mark 16:16)

Why did we hear no report of the seventy million Charismatic Catholics going through the waters of believer's baptism? Simply because they heard 'another gospel'. Though claiming to be born again Spirit-filled Christians, they continue to practise Babylon's occult religion and remain baptised into it, through their unscriptural, pagan, infant baptism.

Of all the warnings given by the Apostle Paul, none carries a greater threat of judgement and damnation than the preaching of 'another gospel':

If anyone, including an angel from heaven, preach any other gospel unto you than that which we have preached unto you, LET HIM BE ACCURSED. (See Gal 1:8).

Not until I renounced and repented of my involvement within the Ecumenical Charismatic Renewal Movement did I come to the place of seeing the deception within the movement. I believe all true followers of the Lord Jesus need to do the same thing and return to preaching the gospel.

According to page 156 of Demos Shakarian's book, 'The Happiest People on Earth', Demos accepted an invitation to the Vatican. There he received official thanks from the Vatican for FGBMFI having reached millions of Roman Catholic laymen. The Vatican NEVER gives thanks to any genuine Bible Preaching Protestant Organisation. For she is the 'woman' who sits upon the scarlet coloured beast, full of names of blasphemy, having seven heads and ten horns. (See Revelation 17:3).

> '*And the woman which thou sawest is that great city, which reigneth over the kings of the earth*' (Rev 17:18)
>
> '*And here is the mind which hath wisdom. The seven heads are seven mountains, on which the woman sitteth*'. (Rev 17:9)

Rome is known world-wide as the city of the seven hills. The 'woman' of chapter seventeen of the book of Revelation is 'Rome', that great city which reigns over the kings of the earth. For nearly two thousand years she has schemed, plotted, tortured and murdered millions upon millions in her attempt to gain spiritual and political world dominion. Now she has changed her tactics and is calling for world peace, unity and reconcilliation. She is a wolf dressed up in sheep's clothing!

Dr Fred Ladenius, a practising Roman Catholic, has been a member of the Vatican Press Office and served under Pope John XXIII and Paul VI. Strangely enough, he is also the editor of 'Voice' Magazine, the FGBMFI's monthly magazine. Apart from testimonies that are recorded monthly, the 'Voice' magazine is also used to express Vatican thoughts and policy for church unity.

'Bridges and not Barriers' was a convention slogan as presented in the September 1981 issue of 'Voice'. It stated:

> 'The long and meaningful relationship between the Fellowship and Roman Catholic believers was expressed after the greetings from a representative of the Most Reverend John, Cardinal Knol, Archbishop of Philadelphia in Father Dean Braun's role as MAIN SPEAKER and the impressive number of Catholic laymen from Philadephia area'.

At the Philadelphia Civic Centre, 20,000 Pentecostals and Charismatics gathered for the 28th World Convention. the applause was deafening as Roman Catholic Father Braun spoke on 'mashed potatoes': the peeling away of the division between Catholic and Protestants and their merging together.

For thirty years the FGBMFI has worked to bring unity between Pentecostals and Catholics and has in effect become a tool of Vatican ecumenism – aiming for unity with the Church of Rome.

As in most circumstances in life, God can turn any situation around and use it for His Glory. There is no doubt that He has used true born-again believers within the movement to draw many to Himself, as in my own case. I re-dedicated my life to Christ at a Full Gospel after-dinner meeting. Yet we cannot overlook the fact that the FGBMFI movement has been used by the spirit of Anti-christ to bring unity between Pentecostals and the 'woman' of the Apocalypse.

The testimony of God's dealing in the life of any one individual can be a great source of faith building for others; but for outreach meetings, testimony must be used in conjunction with the preaching of the Word of God. If they are separated there can be no convicting power of the Holy Spirit and no spiritual rebirth. There are many within the FGBMFI who, in spite of the ruling, take great pains to ensure that the gospel is preached and included in their testimonies; but, sadly, this is not always the case. If they stick to the vision of preaching to businessmen they will fulfil their ministry. Avoiding preaching, because it involves doctrine, negates the very purpose of existing. Thousands of believers have 'fallen away' from serving Christ by overlooking doctrinal differences in the cause of unity.

During a conversation with a dear sister in the Lord the other day, who is, incidentally, an ex Roman Catholic, she explained how she had taken her Father to an FGBMFI dinner in the hope that he would be saved from the bondages of Catholicism. But she was appalled when the speaker produced from his pocket a set of Rosary-beads to prove that he was a good Catholic. She confronted the president at the end of the meeting and showed her disappointment and disapproval. The president brushed the whole issue aside and said, 'Oh but isn't he a lovely man?'

> *'Now the Spirit speaketh expressly that in the latter times some shall depart from the faith, giving heed to seducing spirits, and doctrines of devils; speaking lies in hypocrisy; having their conscience seared with a hot iron.'*
>
> (1 Tim 4:1–2)

The 'last days' apostasy or 'falling away' from the faith is satanic in origin. Its doctrines are doctrines of devils, or demons. Its professors are to be hypocrites and liars, having their consciences seared with a hot iron – men who will lose their conscience against error and sin. Such men would have:

> *' . . . a form of godliness but denying the power thereof: from such turn away.'* (2 Tim 3:5)

These men are not open opponents of the Gospel of Christ. On the contrary, they are great professors, having a form of godliness – a hypocritical form. The apostasy is to be a result of what Paul names ***'the mystery of iniquity'*** (2 Thes 2:7). The iniquity is to be hidden – a mystery – people will not recognise it as iniquity, but will be deceived by it. A form of godliness – a beautiful garment of light covering the form of the prince of darkness.

Within the Ecumenical Charismatic Renewal Movement, of which the FGBMFI is a vital tool in Rome's hand, to break down denominational barriers, especially between Catholicism and Christianity, are to be found those who have a form of godliness, wearing beautiful garments of light, covering the form of the prince of darkness. They are clever imitators of the apostles, great professors of godliness, and are like the magicians of Egypt, who withstood Moses: they did not deny his miracles but counterfeited them.

Within the Ecumenical Charismatic Renewal Movement 'another gospel' is preached, and through this movement we see a revival of Babylon's ancient religion dressed up in beautiful garments of light to look like 'charismatic Christianity' which covers the form of the prince of darkness.

We can see evidence of this at the Vatican Congress on Charismatic Renewal, held in St Peter's Basilica, Rome, which was attended by some leading Full Gospel Businessmen. David du Plessis, an FGBMFI supporter, described the Mass as being a 'Pentecostal Mass with Pentecostal Manifestations'.

I encourage all true followers of Jesus Christ to do as I have done, and repent of, and renounce all involvement within ecumenical circles. The ecumenical demons of deception cause one's conscience to be seared with a hot iron – lose one's conscience against error and sin, and all true spiritual discernment.

Many good, honest, Christ-loving men within the FGBMFI truly believe that the principles of their organisation are strictly non-denominational. Brethren, it is one thing to invite unconverted Catholics to a gospel meeting to hear the Word of

God proclaimed. It is quite another matter to go to a meeting where Roman Catholics and Roman Catholic priests, who claim to be born-again, but still firmly hold to the entire doctrine of Rome, speak from the platform and minister to the unsuspecting, laying hands on them and praying. This situation often arises within FGBMFI circles. Thus we find the answer for the many counterfeit manifestations which promotes spiritual falsehood and lying signs and wonders within the organisation, because those ministering have themselves been deceived by a false gospel and are open to being used.

The 'born-again' experience cannot be achieved by giving mental assent to a theological proposition. As the individual responds to the incorruptible Word of God, God by His Spirit does a supernatural eternal work within the individual, which brings the convicted rebel, who is already judged worthy of eternal damnation, into the intimate relationship of Sonship. This can only come to pass through the Word of God being communicated in such a way as to expose pagan concepts and heretical doctrines. This is what is sadly lacking within all non-denominational organisations who work for unity and overlook doctrinal differences. Not only is it lacking, but is denounced by the heirarchy of such organisations.

Whilst sharing my testimony at an FGBMFI after-dinner meeting in late 1987. I exposed Rome as being the 'woman' of the Apocalypse:

> *'. . . come hither, I will show unto thee the judgement of the great whore that sitteth upon many waters. With whom*

*the kings of the earth have committed fornication and the inhabitions of the earth have been made drunk with the wine of her fornication*'. (Rev 17:1–2)

Some time later I heard through the 'grapevine' that a letter of apology had been sent by the fellowship to every Roman Catholic who had been present at the meeting. As a result of the meeting I received a letter from an International Director of the organisation. The letter included extracts from the chapter manual. These pointed out that one was to . . . 'avoid doctrinal controversy . . . controversial teachings and doctrinal differences should be carefully avoided . . . all remarks about churches, denominations and individuals ought to be edifying, uplifting and complimentary . . .'

The time has come when:

'. . . *they will not endure sound doctrine, but after their own lusts shall they heap to themselves teachers, having itching ears.*

*And they shall turn away their ears from the truth; and shall be turned unto fables.*' (2 Tim 4:3–4)

Today, within non-denominational ecumenical circles we are admonished to preach a gospel that can offend no man. Thousands of believers have 'fallen away' from serving Christ, by refusing to 'contend' for the faith, which was once delivered unto the saints. (Jude v.3)

In spite of great opposition Major Peter Mauldon, president of the Preston Chapter of the FGBMFI invited me to share my testimony at an after-dinner meeting last December. I was to share the testimony of how God had called me to the

Philippines. I included in the testimony the events of my third visit to the Philippines, and explained that God had sent me there to publicly compare the doctrines of the Church of Rome with the Word of God in order that the captives hear the truth, which alone can set them free.

This testimony caused an uproar in the meeting. The Secretary, who was a practising Roman Catholic, walked out. Other practising Roman Catholics responded with shouts of anger before leaving the meeting.

In spite of all the opposition God answered our prayers and confirmed His Word with signs following. The testimony of how God confirmed His Word is here copied from a letter written by Peter, 'Two people were healed of deafness, one of blindness and many others were healed of diverse ailments. Jim Hodsom was jumping around like the man healed through Peter at the gate of the temple, declaring that his foot trouble had gone, and he was praising God, and another man submitted his life to the Lord.'

This particular meeting caused much concern at the International Directors level of the organisation, as I had not submitted to the ruling of 'avoiding doctrinal controversy'. I was accused of creating division in the Body of Christ, by speaking out against the Catholic Church. Finally, the International Director wrote to Peter, advising him to talk to the local Roman Catholic Parish Priest and seek full reconciliation.

Letter dated 3rd February 1988 to Mr Peter Maulden from R.R. Spilman, International Director, FGBMFI:

Dear Peter,

Greetings in the Name of Jesus!

Further to our discussion last night about the visit of Isabel Chapman to your Chapter, I enclose a copy of a letter which was sent to her in December 1986; you will see that we have asked her not to speak against the Catholic Church. Others have spoken to her on the same lines, but she continues to do this and creates division within the Body of Christ as a result.

I am sorry that you were unaware of the situation with regard to Isabel, which has generally been communicated by word of mouth. We always hesitate to put delicate matters of this sort into writing because they can get into the wrong hands, and in any case people can repent and change their ways but a letter continues to exist.

I should be grateful if you would speak with Father Peter Dolan and explain the situation and seek full reconciliation.

Yours in Christ,

Bob.

So there we have it from the horse's mouth so to speak. Anyone who dares to expose Rome's heretical doctrines and satanic practices are looked upon by the hierarchy of the FGBMFI as being divisive and guilty of creating division within the Body of Christ. It is clear for all to see when the organisation speaks of the 'Body of Christ', the Church of Rome is included, in spite of her heretical doctrines.

Jesus rebuked the Church in Pergamos and declared:

*'. . . I have a few things against thee, because thou hast there them that hold the doctrine of Balaam, who taught Balac to cast a stumbling block before the children of Israel, to eat things sacrificed unto idols, and to commit fornication.*

*So hast thou them that hold to the doctrine of the Nicolaitans, which thing I hate.*

*Repent, or else I will come unto thee quickly, and will fight against them with the sword of my mouth.'*

(Rev 2:14–16)

The Lord rebuked the Church at Pergamos for continuing in communion with persons who held to false doctrines and corrupt practises. Such communion in fellowship within the Church draws a guilt and blemish over the whole society, and when God comes to punish the corrupt members of the Church, some drops of the storm fall on the whole society. This land of ours was saved by the Word of God being brought to its shores, and the Reformation saints who fearlessly stood against the deception of Romanism. It became a great nation which enjoyed the blessings of God. Britain today has hardened her heart and will not listen to the truth of her deliverance, she refuses to repent of her fellowship with those who hold to heretical doctrines and corrupt practises. God came and showed this nation the 'tip of the iceberg' of his fury. We experienced a fierce hurricane as the Lord came to punish the corrupt members of the Church. Our trees were uprooted, properties were damaged, television masts were cut down, but still the Church did not respond and purge out from her midst those who hold to heretical doctrines and corrupt practises.

Then came the Stock Exchange panic. Still the Church did not repent, nor purge from her midst those who hold to heretical doctrines and corrupt practises. We have seen disasters in the air, sea and underground, but still the Church refuses to repent and purge out from her midst those who hold to heretical doctrines and corrupt practises.

We have seen a great acceleration in crime, murder, immorality and occultism, but still the Church refuses to purge from her midst those who hold to heretical doctrines and corrupt practises.

The cruel curse of Aids hangs over the heads of untold numbers and innocent babies are born with the deadly disease. Still the Church refuses to purge from her midst those who hold to heretical doctrines and corrupt practises. If the Church in a nation remains faithful to God, He faithfully blesses that nation. If the Church is unfaithful to God, God lifts his cup of blessing from that nation. Unless the Church in Britain repents and purges from her midst those who hold to heretical doctrines and corrupt practises, God will further fight against them, with the sword of His mouth. God's patience with this nation is wearing thin, and unless the Church repents quickly this nation will face the full fury of God's anger.

I was thrilled and overjoyed to receive an FGBMFI circular in my mail, calling the fellowship to a day of repentance, prayer and fasting on March 5th, 1988. But I was horrified to find that the circular was also a subtle expression of Rome's condemnation of those who refuse to bow the knee to her policy of non-denominational unity and peace.

Chapter IV of the FGBMFI circular is an example of the deception of the 'mystery of iniquity' which is so powerfully at work in these end days. The 'iniquity' cannot easily be seen, as it is hidden, and is all part of Satan's master plan to 'unite' the whole of Christendom with Rome and form the 'one world' Apostate, End-time Church. Let us, by the Spirit of God, discern the hidden iniquity in the circular message.

First, let us remember that the organisation acts as an 'arm' of 'the church', which encourages people back into their original denominations, including the Roman Catholic Church, in spite of its unscriptural doctrines and corrupt practises. Through this mode of action, it can be seen that the FGBMFI makes absolutely no distinction between Protestatism and Catholicism – Protestantism being Bible-based, and Catholicism being Satan-inspired. It must also be remembered that the Papacy used exactly the same tactics of infiltration through Billy Graham's ministry. The supposedly new converts were sent back to their original denominations which ensured that Roman Catholics were not drawn into Protestantism. Ultimately, the unsuspecting enquirer's names were given to priests and nuns, who drew them into Rome's web of deception. Another important factor that must not be overlooked is that the Papacy claims that the Roman Catholic Church is the 'one and only true church of Jesus Christ'. Hence the name 'Mystery' Babylon.

> *'And upon her forehead was a name written "Mystery" Babylon the Great, Mother of harlots and abominations of the earth'*. (Rev 17:5)

The true character of Babylon's ancient religion was never concealed, but Roman Catholicism, or paganised Christianity, is a 'mystery' – it is not what it seems. It professes to be divine, but in character is Satanic, thus we have the name 'Mystery Babylon'.

The first 'mystery of iniquity' or 'hidden iniquity' of the FGBMFI circular is that, when the Body of Christ is referred to, the Roman Catholic Church is included and represented:

> Step one of the FGBMFI circular:
> 'Satan is aware of the developments that would bring together the Body of Christ and will do all in his power to prevent it.'

The development that would bring together the Body of Christ is surely Ecumenism – unity between Catholicism and Christianity. Through the movement, vital differences in belief have become blurred; uniting for revival has become the common cry, with any reference to doctrine being discouraged and frowned upon as divisive and unnecessary, as Rome seeks to reverse the Protestant Reformation. We can see how the enemy has twisted the truth to make the 'protestors' of the Ecumenical Movement appear as Satan's agents, who will do all in their power to prevent the developments that would being together the Body of Christ (Catholicism with all other denominations). The genuine unity in the Spirit does not have to be 'brought together'. It's automatic (Ephesians 4).

Step two:

'He has had many ways that have proved successful over the past two thousand years, but one that has been uniquely successful is dividing the Body of Christ – namely the party spirit, or denominational spirit'. (FGBMFI Circular)

Here we see how the work of the Holy Spirit, through those who protested against Romanism, broke away and founded Protestant denominations over the past two thousand years, are made to appear as workers of Satan, guilty of bringing division to the Body of Christ (Catholicism), by a party spirit or denominational spirit.

Step three:

'Its work is to create an exclusive group within the Body of Christ usually on the basis of doctrine. The party spirit is a controlling spirit that keeps those within its group in bondage. Thus true Christians within that group are not open to fellowship with other true Christians locally, so the Body of Christ is divided and largely ineffective.' (FGBMFI Circular)

The Holy Spirit is here accused of being a controlling spirit who holds its people in bondage, through doctrine. This bondage stops true Christians within its group from fellowshipping with other true Christians (Roman Catholics) and is responsible for division in local communities. Those who hold to the doctrine of Christ and refuse to fellowship with Romanists, who 'claim' to be born-again, are responsible for division in local communities, and hinder Rome's efforts of uniting all denominations.

Step four:

'We have recently seen a concerted attack by Satan to maintain such division with anti-Catholic propaganda on the one hand and by attacking the FGBMFI for having fellowship with Roman Catholics on the other. Likewise members of House Fellowships are scathing about the Church of England and vice versa'. (FGBMFI Circular)

The work of the Holy Spirit within these who refuse to compromise with the unscriptural doctrines of Rome are once again accused of doing Satan's work by exposing Roman heresies (anti-Catholic propaganda) on the one hand and attacking the FGBMFI for her fellowship with Romanists on the other. Yet the Word of God declares:

*'Have no fellowship with the unfruitful works of darkness, but rather reprove them'*. (Ephesians 5:11)

Those of us who have expressed disapproval of the FGBMFI's acceptance of the Roman Catholic Church as part of the Body of Christ are again accused of causing division within the Body of Christ. The Church of England and Free Fellowships have also been rebuked by the FGBMFI and accused of being scathing towards each other. No doubt the Free Fellowships are not slow to show their disapproval of the Church of England's moves towards re-uniting with Rome.

Step five:

'In considering our response we remember we are called to judge all things to see if they be true (1 Cor

2:15), but we are not to pass judgement on others or their views'. (FGBMFI Circular)

Let us read the above scripture in its proper Biblical context:

*'But the natural man receiveth not the things of the Spirit of God for they are foolishness unto him: neither can he know them because they are spiritually discerned.*

*But he that is spiritual judgeth all things, yet he himself is judged of no man.*

*For who hath known the mind of the Lord that he may instruct him. But we have the mind of Christ.'*

(1 Corinthians 2:14–15)

The above scripture, when read in the proper context, shows how the spiritual man tries, examines, investigates, inquires into, questions and discerns all things, yet he himself is to be judged of no man, for he has the mind of Christ and is instructed and taught by the Holy Spirit. But the natural man, the unregenerate man cannot receive the things of the Spirit or know them; they are foolishness unto him. The scripture has been used out of context in an attempt to stop any judgement of others or their views, which is a complete contradiction of the Word of God, which reads:

*'Preach the Word; be instant in season, out of season, reprove, rebuke, exhort with all longsuffering and doctrine.*

*For the time will come when they will not endure sound doctrine, but after their own lusts shall they heap to themselves teachers, having itching ears; and they shall turn away their ears from the truth, and shall be turned unto fables!'* (2 Tim 4:2–4)

We are not to preach our own notions and fancies but the pure, plain word of God. We must exhort with patience as the Lord is longsuffering; it must be done rationally, 'not with passion', but with doctrine. We must point out faults and false doctrine in order to bring others to repentance. We have been warned that the time will come when many will not endure sound doctrine. This time has come, and is most evident in FBMFI circles, where 'another gospel' – another means of salvation – is proclaimed.

> Step six:
> 'If we fall into this trap (pass judgement on others or their views) we set ourselves up as the authority – as God – and will be judged accordingly. (Matt 7:1) Thus in speaking to a Christian about the errors of his denomination, we act as judge and are in a place of judgement before God.' (FGBMFI Circular)

In opposition to the Word of God we are once again admonished never to pass judgement or to comment on others or their views. We are not to speak to a Christian (Roman Catholic) about the errors of his denomination. If we walk in obedience to the Word of God – reprove and rebuke error – we are seen as setting ourselves up as God, and will be in a place of judgement before God. The pressure is on. Rome is beginning to show her ugly side. Her greatest method of control always has been and still is, fear!

Now we see her using the FGBMFI as her mouth-piece to shut the mouths of true believers by putting them in bondage of 'fear of God's judgement', if they speak against the errors of Catholicism or any other denominations. Choose this day whom ye shall serve; Rome via the FGBMFI, or the Holy Scriptures.

> *'Brethren, if any of you do err from the truth, and one convert him, let him know that he which converteth the sinner from the error of his way, shall save a soul from death and shall cover a multitude of sins.'* (James 5:20)

> Step seven:
> 'The hearer will reject our judgement and most likely recede condemned into his denominational group, thus creating a deeper division in the Body of Christ. We have done what Satan wants' (FGBMFI Circular)

Such a statement is subtle, evil manipulation to prevent error being exposed. Those who rebuke and reprove error are accused of doing the work of Satan by causing division in the body of Christ.

> Step eight:
> 'Jesus came not to judge the world, but to save it (John 12:47–48); this must be our response.' (FGBMFI Circular)

Jesus did say, ***'I came not to judge the world but to save the world'***; he also said:

> *'I am come as a light into the world that whosoever believeth on me should not abide in darkness. And if any man hear my words and believe not, I judge him not: for I came not to judge the world but to save the world. He that rejecteth me and receive not my words have ONE that judgeth him. THE WORD that I have spoken, the same shall judge him in the last day.'* (John 12:47–48)

God is longsuffering, not willing that any should perish, therefore he sends his servants to proclaim his Word, which exposes error. According to the circular, those who expose error are accused of 'judging' others. In actual fact, it is the Word that judges them, and all who continue to reject His Word will finally be eternally damned by it, on the last day.

> 'It is the Word of God that when spoken under the anointing of God brings light and truth (Psalm 119:130). Those who abide in the Word shall know the truth, and the truth shall set them free. (John 8:31–32). We must not therefore speak against denominations or their doctrines – but speak the Word of God. This will achieve by spiritual means those things we can never achieve by natural means.' (FGBMFI Circular)

On calculating evil 'mystery of iniquity'! Here the FGBMFI clearly acknowledges that natural means cannot achieve spiritual things. Like Rome she claims adherence to the Word of God, but in actual fact, except in rare instances the 'preaching of scripture' is forbidden in the after dinner meetings. How can these spiritual things be achieved, when they use only the natural means – man's testimony – man's words?

It is terrible but true; regardless of how good one's intentions are, or how much one claims to love the Lord, any Christian who is involved within ecumenical circles is unwittingly helping to build the Church of Anti-christ, serving the Pope's objectives of a one world church under Rome. Multitudes of believers have 'fallen away' from serving

Christ and instead serve the Pope – the head of the Church of Anti-christ.

I weep, mourn and groan in my spirit for 'the Church' in this nation. She hears God's call to repent but refuses to listen to the truth of her deliverance. She arranges special days of prayer and fasting where she 'stands in the gap' and repents of the sins of the unregenerate population of the nations.

She does not understand that judgement begins in the House of God. She cannot see the error of her own evil ways and unfaithfulness to God and His Word!

Instead of repenting of her own sins, she repents of the sins of others, therefore the judgements of God continue. Instead of purging the corrupt members of the Church out from her midst, she obeys the spirit of iniquity and repents of division!

Her own conscience has been seared by a hot iron – she is losing her conscience against error and sin!

She listens to the mystery of iniquity and refuses to reprove and rebuke error, which grieves the Holy Ghost!

She is used by Anti-christ to promote 'another gospel', another way of salvation!

She helps promote the works of Anti-christ by not voicing her disapproval of heretical doctrines and corrupt practises.

She stands on Anti-christ's side and rebukes those who rebuke, reprove and expose error.

She stands on Anti-christ's side against the work of the Holy Ghost during the Reformation, by keeping silent and not voicing her disapproval of heretical doctrines and corrupt practises.

She stands on Anti-christ's side by calling for an end to all division, and helps the enemy build and unite his counterfeit bride.

She slays the hand which brought her light and liberty, she stands on Anti-christ's side and helps promote the work which aims to reverse the Protestant Reformation.

She has 'fallen away' from serving Christ, and now helps the beast heal his deadly wound.

Hear the Word of the Lord:

*'Repent or else I will come unto thee quickly and will fight against them with the sword of my mouth.'* (Rev 2:16)

*'Suppose ye that I am come to give peace on earth? I tell you, Nay, but rather division. For from hence forth there shall be five in one house divided, three against two and two against three.*

*The father shall be divided against the son, and the son against the father; the mother against the daughter, and the daughter against the mother; the mother-in-law against her daughter-in-law, the daughter-in-law against her mother-in-law'* (Luke 12:51–53)

All true born-again believers are called upon to ***'contend for the faith once delivered unto the saints.'*** (Jude v.3)

To be – ***'set for the defence of the gospel'*** (Phil 1:7)
To – ***'put on the whole armour of God!'*** (Eph 6:11)
To – ***'fight the good fight of faith'*** (1 Tim 6:12)
To – ***'enter into spiritual warfare for the cause of Jesus Christ'*** (Eph 6:12).

To stand for truth and oppose error, to promote righteousness and expose sin. The present day believer is required to be as committed to the great cause of Christ as those who have been martyred for their faith throughout the generations. The martyrs would not have died for the faith had they been more ecumenical in their methods of evangelism, as many of today's Christians are.

Was Jeremiah wrong because he called the nation to repent?

Was Amos wrong because he exposed the compromise and disobedience of God's people?

Was Elijah wrong because he was a 'troubler of Israel'?

Was the Lord Jesus wrong when he denounced the Scribes and Pharisees? (Matt 23)

Surely not!

To contend for the faith by opposing error, which exposes sin, will cost a faithful Christian a great deal of persecution, disapproval, and even death.

The Apostle Paul suffered a great deal of persecution and was finally beheaded. He sealed his testimony with his blood, having no fear of death.

Had Paul been less controversial for the cause of Christ, and more ecumenical, he would probably never have had to face such persecution or cruel death. Not counting the cost of self he proclaimed, ***'I am not ashamed of the Gospel of Christ'***. He might just as well have said, 'I am not ashamed to engage in controversy for the Gospel of Christ!'.

This, my brethren, is the position in which I stand, 'I am not ashamed to engage in controversy for the cause of the Gospel of Christ!'

Like all true, Bible-believing Christians, I promote and advocate love, unity and peace amongst

God's people, but not at the price of compromise. You cannot trade Biblical truth for superficial 'unity'.

My only motive for engaging in controversy is to defend the faith, expose error and present Biblical Christianity to a lost and dying world, knowing that:

> *'he which converteth the sinner from the error of his ways, shall save a soul from hell.'* (James 5:20)

## References

1. Chick Publications, PO Box 662, Chino, California CA91710 USA

# *Chapter 7*

# The Spirit of Truth

> *'Whosoever transgresseth, and abideth not in the doctrine of Christ, hath not God'* (2 John 9)

Those who do not abide in the doctrine of Christ nor remain content with that which Jesus taught – do not have God – therefore cannot be born of God's Spirit.

The Holy Spirit is the Spirit of truth. He is the true believer's guide and teacher. He has undertaken to lead those whom He indwells into all truth.

> *'When he the spirit of truth is come, he will guide you into all truth'* (John 16:13)

Part of the Holy Spirit's work in the life of a believer is to lead and guide into truth. He shall teach nothing but the truth. As the skilful pilot guides the ship into the port for which it is bound, so the Holy Spirit leads the believer along the narrow way, ensuring that the believer abides in the doctrine of Christ and does not fall short of his goal.

This does not mean that believers become infallible; on the contrary; we make many mistakes and jump to wrong conclusions, usually through a lack of knowledge of the Word of God. Yet those who are truly born of God's Spirit cannot remain in error, for the work of the Holy Spirit in the life of any one individual is to lead into all truth.

So what are we to believe of those who claim to be born-again, filled with the Holy Spirit and power, and speak in tongues, but continue in error and false doctrines? According to the Holy Scriptures they 'hath not God'; therefore, they have not been born-again by the incorruptible Word of God.

This, brethren, is a good doctrinal test to be applied to those who claim to be born-again.

> *'Whosoever transgresseth and abideth not in the doctrine of Christ, hath not God. He that abideth in the doctrine of Christ, he hath both the Father and the son.*
>
> *If there come any unto you and bring not this doctrine, receive him not into your house, neither bid him God speed.*
>
> *For he that biddeth him God speed is partaker of his evil deeds.'* (2 John 9–11)

Those who are truly born-again of God's Spirit will abide in the doctrine of Christ, being completely satisfied and fulfilled with that which Jesus taught.

In these end days in which we live, the Holy Spirit is preparing the Bride of Christ to stand and endure the persecution which looms on the horizon. Like the true saints that have gone before us, many of our number will be faced with death as a result of our faithfulness to the doctrine of Christ and refusal to compromise with the church of Anti-christ. Yet some of our number will survive and be:

> *' . . . caught up together with them in the clouds to meet the Lord in the air.'* (1 Thess 4:16)

Oh what a day that shall be! the kingdoms of this world will become The Kingdoms of our Lord and

His Christ, and he shall reign for ever and ever. (See Revelation 11:15).

Before the Lord establishes his kingdom of peace on earth, He will first pour forth his wrath on the rebellious inhabitants of the earth as is recorded in chapter sixteen of the book of Revelation. Satan will be stripped of his power as Prince of this world and cast into the bottomless pit for one thousand years. See Rev 20:1–3.

## Christ's 1,000 Year Reign of Peace

*'And the Lord shall be king over all the earth: in that day there shall be one Lord, and his name one.'* (Zech 14:9)

*'But with righteousness shall he judge the poor, and reprove with equity for the meek of the earth: and he shall smite the earth with the rod of his mouth, and with the breath of his lips shall he slay the wicked.*

*And righteousness shall be the girdle of his loins, and faithfulness the girdle of his reins.*

*The wolf also shall dwell with the lamb, and the leopard shall lie down with the kid; and the calf and the young lion and the fatling together; and a little child shall lead them.*

*And the cow and the bear shall feed; their young ones shall lie down together: and the lion shall eat straw like the ox.*

*And the suckling child shall play on the hole of the asp, and the weaned child shall put his hand on the cockatrice' den.*

*They shall not hurt nor destroy in all my holy mountain: for the earth shall be full of the knowledge of the Lord, as the waters cover the sea.'* (Isaiah 11:5–9)

*'And it shall come to pass, that every one that is left of all the nations which came against Jerusalem shall even go up from year to year to worship the King, the Lord of hosts, and to keep the feast of tabernacles.*

*And it shall be, that whosoever will not come up of all the families of the earth unto Jerusalem to worship the King, the Lord of hosts, even upon them shall be no rain.*

*And if the family of Egypt go not up, and come not, that have no rain; there shall be the plague, wherewith the Lord will smite the heathen that come not up to keep the feast of tabernacles.*

*This shall be the punishment of Egypt, and the punishment of all nations that come not up to keep the feast of tabernacles.'* (Zechariah 14:16–19)

The Jews and the inhabitants of the earth who survive the wrath of God will enjoy a thousand years of complete peace. Those of us who remain faithful to the doctrine of Christ in this body of the flesh shall rule with Jesus during His coming one thousand year reign of peace. (See Rev 2:26 and Rev 20:6).

Although the earth and its inhabitants will enjoy a thousand years of peace free from all satantic influence, it will still not be the perfect age. There will be those who will rebel against the Lord's call to attend the yearly Feast of Tabernacles. God has given man the divine gift of free will, and even during the coming one thousand years of peace there will be those who will deliberately pursue the way of self-will. The rebellious children will refuse to attend the yearly feast, which will result in God withholding the rain from their crops; though they will not be able to disrupt the order and harmony of Christ's reign.

At the end of the thousand years Satan will be let out of his prison for the last time. The rebellious children will yield to him, and he will lead them on a march against Jerusalem.

> *'And when the thousand years are expired, Satan shall be loosed out of his prison,*
>
> *And shall go out to deceive the nations which are in the four quarters of the earth, Gog and Magog, to gather them together to battle: the number of whom is as the sand of the sea.*
>
> *And they went up on the breadth of the earth, and compassed the camp of the saints about, and the beloved city: and fire came down from God out of heaven, and devoured them.*
>
> *And the devil that deceived was cast into the lake of fire and brimstone, where the beast and the false prophet are, and shall be tormented day and night for ever and ever.'*
>
> (Revelation 20:7–10)

At that time the ungodly dead of all generations will stand before the Judgement Throne of God, only to be cast into the Lake of Fire. Death and hell will be cast into the Lake of Fire. Those who lived and died during Christ's one thousand year reign and remained faithful to the Lord shall be raised from the dead and clothed in their new immortal bodies. (See Rev 20:11–15).

The new heaven and the new earth will then usher in the perfect eternity, the former things will be remembered no more. In that wonderful, wonderful day God Himself will dwell with us: the fellowship that God had with man in the garden of Eden before the fall will be fully restored.

*'And I saw a new heaven and a new earth: for the first heaven and the first earth were passed away; and there was no more sea.*

*And I John saw the holy city, new Jerusalem, coming down from God out of heaven, prepared as a bride adorned for her husband.*

*And I heard a great voice out of heaven saying, Behold, the tabernacle of God is with men, and he will dwell with them, and they shall be his people, and God himself shall be with them, and be their God.*

*And God shall wipe away all tears from their eyes; and there shall be no more death, neither sorrow, nor crying, neither shall there be any more pain: for the former things are passed away.*

*And he that sat upon the throne said, Behold, I make all things new.*

*And he said unto me, Write: for these words are true and faithful.*

*And he said unto me, It is done. I am Alpha and Omega, the beginning and the end. I will give unto him that is athirst of the fountain of the water of life freely.*

*He that overcometh shall inherit all things; and I will be his God, and he shall be my son.'* (Rev 21:1–7)

At present Satan is still Prince of this world: while the Holy Spirit prepares the Bride of Christ for the coming persecution and the 'catching up' of those who survive the persecution, the spirit of Anti-christ is at one and the same time preparing Satan's bride, and a great world wide revival is expected. This is right on target for the Word of God declares:

*'And all that dwell upon the earth shall worship him, whose names are not written in the book of life of the Lamb slain from the foundation of the world'* (Rev 13:8)

Events point to the fact that the Prince of this world is busy mobilising his principalities, powers and spiritual wickedness in high places, to unite his counterfeit bride, for he has been busy on many fronts.

Satan's bride will be a counterfeit of the true Bride of Christ, and will look like the real thing. We are to expect Satan's counterfeit bride to counterfeit all nine gifts of the Holy Spirit. However, one thing we can be sure of, Satan's bride will NOT abide in the doctrine of Christ, she will 'claim' adherence to the Word of God, but will violate it with added false doctrines.

Events point to the fact that apart from uniting his counterfeit bride, Satan also seeks to counterfeit Jesus Christ's coming reign of peace, when He shall rule the world from Jerusalem.

## New Age of Peace and Prosperity

Millions of unregenerate people are actively engaged in the 'New Age Movement', which consists of tens of thousands of co-operating organisations within a world wide network. The leaders of the movement claim to have worldwide powerful influence, boasting that they have infiltrated every level of society, with conspirators in every department of government, in all areas of policy making, in volunteer organisations, corporations, universities, hospitals and factories.

The main thrust of the movement's teaching is that man is about to enter into a new state of evolution, where mankind will discover that they are all gods. As man enters into this new phase of evolution it will enable him to live in complete harmony with his brothers. The result will be that a beautiful new world will emerge – a world without suffering, where war and famine will be a thing of the past, everyone will share and no-one will go hungry – an ecumenical world where there will be no division over religion or doctrine. Everyone will believe in one god – everyone will respect each other's ways of worshipping god. The Buddhist will accept that Mary is the Roman Catholic's way to God, the Roman Catholics will accept that Buddha is the Buddhist's way to God, and so on.

Followers of the New Age movement are being brainwashed into accepting a one world religion and a one world government. For further information on the New Age Movement, see 'Understanding the New Age' by Roy and Rae Livesey, published by New Wine Press.

New Agers are actively involved in many Satanic practises, but here we will mention only a few; evolution, spiritism, yoga, transcendental meditation and witchcraft. Many claim to be Christians but they certainly do not abide in the doctrine of Christ, therefore – hath not God. Yet they promote many 'good works programmes' such as disarmament campaigns, hunger relief programmes, Live Aid, world day of prayer, peace movements, whole earth catalogues and many other social and humanistic causes. The New Age Movement should not be underestimated but seen as part of Satan's ecumenical plan to unite mankind under one spiritual leader and one world government.

Using methods such as holistic health centres, inner healing which includes visualisation, mind control courses, yoga, transcendental meditation, hunger relief programmes, disarmament campaigns and peace movements, Satan has led many nominal Christians into occult practises, thereby bringing them under the control of demons of deception. These well-meaning but deceived people become Satan's agents and help in the work of building the counterfeit bride and New World of peace, unity and brotherhood.

## Yet Another Harlot Daughter

New Agers are not alone in their ambition to build a new world of peace, unity and brotherhood.

Leaders of the House Church Movement also teach of a new world of peace and prosperity. Are they faithfully abiding in the doctrine of Christ? Can their 'Kingdom Now' doctrine, of a new world of peace and prosperity be substantiated by the Word of God?

Leaders of the House Church Movement teach that they, and their followers, have the power to overcome the forces of evil and take dominion over all governments, law and legislation. Their goal is to take over the world and establish the Kingdom of God on EARTH. Once this has been accomplished they expect to see Jesus return, not to 'catch us up' but return to earth to rule over the kingdom which THEY will have established for Him.

In the eyes of New Agers and globalists, the key to a binding political, economic unity, is the formation of a one world religion. According to the New Agers, this one world religion will be a synthesis of all the world's faiths, who have compromised around the theme, 'we are the world – we are all gods'.

However, while 'Kingdom Now' theology believers agree that political and economic unity is necessary and desirable, they agree that the one world religion which will bind it all together will be a revised, powerful, authoritative brand of Christianity. Their vision of a coming new age of peace and prosperity is identical to that of New Agers and globalists, except for the make-up of the one world religion.

'Kingdom Now' theology preachers teach: 'There will be no great falling away of believers into apostasy'. Yet the Holy Scriptures clearly teach:

> *'Let no man deceive you by any means for that day (day of the Lord's coming) shall not come, except there come a falling away first, and that man of sin be revealed, the son of perdition'.* (2 Thes 2:3)

Are they abiding in the doctrine of Christ? The 'catching up' of believers to meet the Lord in the air, and the subsequent pouring forth of God's wrath upon the inhabitants of the earth, who rejected the truth and believing lies, has no place in the 'Kingdom Now' theology, the theology of a new world of peace and prosperity.

In his book, 'What on Earth is this Kingdom?'[1], a leading figure of the House Church movement refers to the 'catching up' of believers as being ridiculous – ridiculous for at least two reasons. Firstly, the 'catching up' of believers to precede the second coming of Christ was unknown to the biggest majority of the saints during the history of the New Testament Church; also that the theory of the 'catching up' of believers originated around 1830. Evidence of this fact could be read in Dave MacPhersons book, 'The Incredible Cover-up' published by Logos International.[1] The writer fails to realise that Dave MacPherson never suggested that the Rapture would not occur, but that the theory of a secret pre-Tribulation Rapture, before the appearing of the 'man of sin', had its origins around 1830. This new teaching was looked upon by Bible scholars of that day with intolerance, as those promoting it held no respect for the view that had held the field for 1,800 years. In actual fact MacPherson has been misquoted.

Secondly, the writer sees the 'catching up' of believers as being a ridiculous theory, as it has rendered the Church here on earth ineffective, in that the Church's hopes of victory in Christ are in some future date instead of here and now. Finally the writer writes off the 'catching up' of believers as being nothing more nor less than a stretch of the imagination – a fairy tale; an evil theory which allows others to suffer and be tortured while we escape in the air.

Regardless of what the leaders of the House Church movement teach, the Word of God declares:

*'Then we which are alive and remain shall be caught up together with them in the clouds, to meet the Lord in the air; and so shall we ever be with the Lord'* (1 Thes 4:17)

*'Behold I show you a mystery, we shall not all sleep (die) but we shall all be changed, in a moment, in the twinkling of an eye, at the last trump; for the trumpet shall sound and the dead shall be raised incorruptible; and we shall all be changed.*

*For this corruptible must put on incorruption, and this mortal must put on immortality.'* (1 Cor 15:51–53)

As true believers we rejoice that our hope is not of this world.

*'For here have we have no continuing city, but we seek one to come.'* (Hebrews 13:14)

'Kingdom Now' preachers seek to change our heaven-bound hope to an earth-based hope. Jesus clearly taught that just prior to His coming in the clouds, true believers will be hated, persecuted and killed, all over the world. Those of us who will survive the persecution will be 'caught up' into the clouds to meet our Saviour in the air. Then God will pour forth His wrath upon those who rejected the truth and were responsible for the persecution and murder of His faithful saints.

The heirarchic structure and dictatorship of the Shepherding Discipleship and Restoration movements is very similar to that of the the heirarchic structure and dictatorship of Catholicism. The heirarchy of the movements set themselves up as gods over the ordinary folks who have to submit to their covering and direction in all important decisions.

The Church of Rome sets up Mary as mediator for her followers; within the Restoration movements the leaders take Jesus' place as mediator for their followers, the ordinary folks being unable to hear clearly from God in important matters. Rome has perverted the Lord's table with the sacrifice of the Mass. The Restoration Movements have perverted the Lord's table with their 'covenant commitment' doctrine, which is supposed to bind followers and leaders together in an agreement of commitment to one other, denying the overiding prime relationship to God and personal responsibilities.

The 'Kingdom Now' theology preachers teach that God has forever cast the children of Israel away from Himself, and the reborn state of Israel has no prophetic significance. The physical descendants of Abraham, Isaac and Jacob have no future hope as a distinct people. All the covenant promises made to the children of Israel have been forfeited and given permanently to 'the Church'. They claim to be spiritual Israel – the New Jerusalem. Once again we can see that such a teaching is a complete contradiction to the Word of God:

> *'For I would not, brethren, that ye should be ignorant of this mystery, lest ye should be wise in your own conceits; that blindness in part is happened to Israel until the fulness of the Gentiles be come in. And so all Israel shall be saved, as it is written, there shall come out of Sion the Deliverer, and shall turn away ungodliness from Jacob: For this is my covenant unto them, when I shall take away their sins. As concerning the gospel, they are enemies for your sakes: but as touching the election, they are beloved for the father's sake. For the gifts and calling of God are without repentance'.* (Romans 11:25–29)

True born-again believers are Abraham's seed and heirs according to the promise, through the circumcision of the heart. Being the branch that was grafted in they do not boast against the root that brought them light. For if God spared not the natural branch we need to take heed lest he spare not us, for we stand by faith alone. (See Romans Chapter 11).

What of the Shepherding, Discipleship and Restoration movements who claim they have replaced the natural branch? Surely they are wise in their own conceits. Let us turn to the book of Revelation and see how God looks upon those who claim to be Jews or the 'New Jerusalem' but are not:

> *' . . . I know the blasphemy of them which say they are Jews, and are not, but are the synagogue of Satan'*
>
> (Revelation 2:9)

The Holy Spirit is the Spirit of Truth, who leads us into all truth. The spirit behind the 'Kingdom Now' theology teaching cannot possibly be the Holy Spirit. Those who hold to such unscriptural doctrines are not abiding in the doctrine of Christ therefore 'hath not God'.

> *Repent; or else I will come unto thee quickly, and will fight against them with the sword of my mouth.'*
>
> (Revelation 2:16)

> *'Not every one that saith unto me, Lord, Lord, shall enter into the kingdom of heaven: but he that doeth the will of my father which is in heaven'* (Matt 7:21)

It will not suffice to say, Lord! Lord! in word and tongue, or make address or profession of Christ as our master! Having a form of godliness is not enough to bring one into the Kingdom of Heaven. To enter into the Kingdom of Heaven, it is necessary to do the will of Christ, which is the will of His Father in Heaven. The Father's will is that we believe in the Lord Jesus, that we walk in obedience to His Word, repent of sin and error and have no fellowship with those who hold to heretical doctrines; that we live a holy life of faith and love one another. Saying and doing are two different matters.

> *'Many will say unto me in that day, Lord, Lord, have we not prophesied in thy name? and in they name have cast out devils? and in thy name done many wonderful works'*
> (Matt 7:22)

Hypocrites will offer the Lord other things in lieu of obedience; with great confidence they will say unto the Lord:

'Lord, don't you know we have prophesied in thy name?'

They may have prophesied in His name, but He did not send them: they made 'use' of His Name to serve their own purposes.

'Lord, don't you know we cast out devils in Your Name?'

Judas cast out devils, yet he was a son of perdition.

'Lord, don't you know we have done many wonderful works in Your Name?'

Wonderful works will never gain a man entry into Heaven, for by grace are ye saved through faith alone. Repentance, grace, love, a holy life of faith and obedience to the Word of God, is the way of salvation.

*'And then I will profess unto them, I never knew you: depart from me, ye that work iniquity'* (Matt 7:23)

The Lord will reject them on the grounds that He knew them only as hypocritical workers of iniquity. Therefore let every one that names the name of Christ, depart from iniquity.

## Post-Millenial Teaching

Satan could not possibly have pulled off a greater or more effective plan of deception than to get the House Church Movement to believe the post-millenial teaching (meaning they believe the millenium thousand years of peace will occur before Christ returns). Through this unscriptural teaching the House Church Movement is seeking to mobilise its followers to rise up and take political control of the world and bring in the 'Kingdom of God' upon the earth.

Restorationists believe that Christ's coming altered ceremonial law, and put an end to animal sacrifices, but anticipate a day when they will govern the World using the Old Testament as their law book. Such teaching causes the sacrifice of Jesus Christ to be of no effect, and is every bit as blasphemous as Rome's doctrine of penance, because, we are saved by grace through faith – not by Old Testament law.

Pat Robertson, a leading American preacher of the Restoration Movement in the United States, sees a 'Utopia' brought about by Christian rule. He sees a school system where humanism isn't taught anymore, a world in which there are no more abortions, where juvenile delinquency is virtually unknown, where the prisons are virtually empty, a society where church members have taken dominion over the forces of the World, where Satan's power is bound by the people of God, a world where there is no more disease or demon possession. He is persuaded that we are standing on the brink of the greatest spiritual revival the world has ever known. He sees hundreds of millions of people coming into the Kingdom in the next several years.

What a wonderful vision; we would all love to live in a practically sin-free world. The truth is, however, this present world is under a curse and cannot be restored to perfection in this present era. In Romans 8:18–23, Paul links the deliverance of this physical world with the redemption of the Christian's body – the resurrection – which takes place at the second coming of Jesus.

Spiritual revival does not come by political and social force or reform, neither can it come from exaltation of mankind to the status of being gods. Political and social reforms cannot change man's heart nature of depravity. Only the grace of God can do that. Restorationists look to the law, which they call Biblical principles, as a blueprint for social change. Surely they are under a strong delusion!

> '*. . . if there had been a law given which could have given life, verily righteousness should have been seen by the law*' (Gal 3:21)

*'No man is justified by the law in the sight of God, it is evident: for the just shall live by faith.'* (Gal 3:12)

The whole point of the sacrifice of Jesus was that the law was unable to save mankind. Regardless of what scripture teaches, Restorationists plan to rule the world by the Old Testament law. This new order of Government has been likened to Israel under the reign of King David. The Davidic Kingdom with its rule of law, its king, city and temple, its formalised worship and its dominion over the nations is said to be symbolic of the 'Kingdom of God on Earth'. They believe in three covenants, the Old, the New and the Davidic; the latter being 'a special provision for the Church in these last days'.[2] Are they abiding in the doctrine of Christ?

Jesus said:

*'Verily, verily, I say unto you, I am the door of the sheep'* (John 10:7)

*' . . . He that entereth not by the door into the sheepfold, but climbeth up some other way, the same is a thief and a robber'* (John 10:1)

*'I am the door: by me is any man enter in he shall be saved . . .'* (John 10:9)

The above scriptures clearly teach that Jesus Christ alone is the door of the sheep. Yet Restoration literature teaches that entry into the 'Kingdom' is through the door of the 'elders' – as Jesus is not now physically on earth the church leaders replace Him in this function.[3] To become a disciple in the 'Restoration Kingdom' one must be willing to enter in through one's elder as the 'door' of the sheep.

*'They profess that they know God: but in works they deny Him, being abominable, and disobedient, and unto every good work reprobate'* (Titus 1:16)

By replacing Christ as the 'door' of the sheep, leaders of the House Church and Restoration movements rob Jesus of His position as the one and only Saviour of the world.

By replacing Christ as 'mediator' for their followers they deny that Jesus Christ is the one and only mediator of the New Covenant.

They even deny the Everlasting Covenant, claiming that the Davidic Covenant is a special provision of God for the Church in the last days.[4]

They deny the blessed Holy Spirit of His position and ministry in the Church – the leaders stand accountable for the souls of each member in his fold.[5]

We were warned:

*'For there shall arise false Christs, and false prophets, and shall show great signs and wonders, insomuch that, if it were possible, they shall, deceive the very elect.'*

(Matthew 24:24)

To become a disciple of Christ and enter into the Kingdom of God one must be:

*' . . . born of water and of the Spirit . . .'* (John 3:5)

To become a disciple of the 'Restoration Kingdom' one must be willing to submit to one's elders as the 'door' into the Kingdom.

Two different 'kingdoms' with two separate ways of entry.

It must be concluded that within the House Church and Restoration movements, another way of salvation is taught.

They may profess with their mouth that Jesus is the Christ, they may speak in tongues and perform signs and wonders, but in works they deny Him.

*'Who is a liar but he that denieth that Jesus is the Christ? He is anti-christ that denieth the Father and the Son.'*

(1 John 2:22)

They deny the Father and the Son by not abiding in the doctrine of Christ.

*'Whosoever transgresseth, and abideth not in the doctrine of Christ, HATH NOT GOD . . .'* (2 John 9)

Restorationists believe that they have rediscovered the proper Biblical church order, but in actual fact, their church order is a blueprint of the heirarchic Dictatorship of Romanism. Through the spread of the proper church order, they expect the majority of mankind to submit to God's rule, which will bring righteousness and peace to the whole world, before Jesus returns.

Whilst still 'officially' outside the fold of the Church of Rome, Restorationists enjoy genuine fellowship with Roman Catholics and clergy.[6]

Doctrinal differences do not hinder fellowship: doctrinal or behavioural conformity is not necessary to love one another[7] is the cry of Rome's harlot daughters. To those who have unwittingly been drawn into this web of deception, hear what the Spirit is saying to the Church, and 'come out of her, my people'.

God's Word clearly shows, that preceding the coming of Jesus Christ from Heaven to rule this earth, there will be a revival of evil, not of good, which will result in the wrath of God being poured forth upon the children of disobedience. The wicked kingdom comes first; the man of sin will be revealed, before the coming of the Lord Jesus Christ.

> *'Let no man deceive you by any means: for that day shall not come, except there come a falling away first, and that man of sin be revealed, the son of perdition;'* (2 Thes 2:3)

Addressing Jewish, Moslem, Hindu, Buddhist, Sikh, Shinto, Anglican and other faiths at the Assisi World Day of Prayer, the Pope stated:

> 'Our prayers here in Assisi should include repentance for our failure as Christians to carry out the mission of peace and reconciliation that we have received from Christ and which we have not fully accomplished.'

For one day Assisi became the spiritual capital of world peace and unity. One hundred and fifty world religious leaders offered up prayers for peace, according to individual traditional rites.

The Pope addressed the representatives of 150 religions as 'Christians', regardless of their religious beliefs and pagan practises. Therefore it can be concluded that when he refers to the 'Body of Christ' he means the unified faiths of the world.

Revival! Revival! Revival! is the cry of Satan's counterfeit bride. I believe that the 'world day of prayer at Assisi' was the beginning of the 'bringing together' of Satan's counterfeit bride.

As the Church of Anti-christ unites it can be seen to be taking on the appearance of a great world wide revival. Many who claim to be born-again but do not abide in the doctrine of Christ, are performing great counterfeit signs and wonders. These supernatural manifestations are so convincing that they could deceive even the elect – if it were possible, and are fulfilling:

*'Even him (Anti-christ) whose coming is after the working of Satan with all power and signs and lying wonders'*

(2 Thess 2:9)

Brethren, let us look up, for our redemption draws nigh; and take comfort from our Saviour's words:

*' . . . that which ye have already, hold fast till I come. And he that overcometh and keepeth my works unto the end, to him will I give power over the nations.*

*And he shall rule them with a rod of iron; as the vessels of a potter shall be broken to shivers: even as I have received of my father.*

*And I will give him the morning star. He that hath an ear let him hear what the spirit saith unto the churches.'* (Rev 2:25–29)

*'To him that overcometh will I grant to sit with me in my throne, even as I also overcame, and am sat down with my Father in his throne.'* (Rev 3:21)

True saints of God are heaven bound for the Holy Kingdom, not earth-based.

*'He that loveth his life shall lose it; and he that hateth his life in this world shall keep it unto life eternal.'*

(John 12:25)

# References

1. Page 35–36 *What on Earth is This Kingdom?*
2. *Built to Last* by Roy Trudinger.
3. *Built to Last* by Roy Trudinger page 116.
4. *Built to Last* by Roy Trudinger pages 22–29.
5. *Built to Last* by Roy Trudinger page 117.
6. *What on Earth is this Kingdom?* by Gerald Coates page 145.
7. *What on Earth is this Kingdom?* by Gerald Coates page 140–141.

# Chapter 8

# The Woman of the Apocalypse

*'Come hither, and I will shew thee the judgement of the great whore that sitteth upon many waters.'* (Rev 17:1)

A whore, in the natural sense, is a woman who sells her body for financial gain. The woman of the Apocalypse is a 'spiritual' whore, who sells her body (followers) into eternal damnation for financial gain. This can be seen in Rome's doctrine of purgatory; the people pay the priests money, for a hopefully quick exit out of the tormenting flames of purgatory.

*'With whom the kings of the earth have committed fornication, and the inhabitants of the earth have been made drunk with the wine of her fornication'* (Rev 17:2)

The woman of the Apocalypse has deceived even the kings, the rulers of the earth, with her doctrines of deception and caused them to commit spiritual fornication. The inhabitants of the earth have been made drunk – spiritually intoxicated. They are incapable of discerning the difference between truth and error, and are in a state of spiritual confusion, because of her doctrines of deception.

*'So he carried me away in the spirit into the wilderness: and I saw a woman sit upon a scarlet coloured beast, full of names of blasphemy, having seven heads and ten horns.'* (Rev 17:3)

Here we see a picture of the woman of the Apocalypse, the spiritual whore, sit upon a scarlet coloured beast, full of 'names' of blasphemy, having seven heads and ten horns.

## Names of Blasphemy

When the Papal tiara is placed upon the head of a new Pope, the following words are spoken:

> 'Receive this triple crown and know that thou art the father of princes, and the king and ruler of the world.'

The proud tiara of the Papacy symbolizes her power on 'earth' and in 'heaven' and in 'hell'. In all three the Pope claims to rule, which is represented by his triple crown.

Cardinals and chief princes of the church adore His Holiness upon their bended knees, they kiss his right hand and even his feet.

At the coronation, they set him on the high altar of St Peter and adore him as the representative of Deity. He is far above all kings, he is the viceregent of God, the regent of the universe. He is carried in a lofty state on man's shoulders beneath a canopy hung with gold fringes. He is the head of the universal church. He wears the keys as the sign of his power to open the gates of heaven to all believers.

On the occasion of Pope Innocent X's coronation the following words were addressed to him by one of the Cardinals:

> 'Most Holy and Blessed Father, head of the church, ruler of the world, to whom the Keys of the the

> Kingdom of Heaven are committed, whom the angels in heaven adore, and the gates of hell fear, and all the world adores, we especially venerate, worship and adore thee.'

He holds two swords as judging things temporal and spiritual. He is the sole and supreme judge of man, and can himself be judged of no man.

In the Bull Unam Sanctum, Pope Boniface declared:

> 'The Roman Pontiff judges all men but is judged by none . . . we declare, assert and pronounce to be subjects to the Roman Pontiffs to every creature, necessary for salvation . . . I have the authority of the king of kings. I am all in all and above all, so that God Himself, and I, the Vicar of God, have but one consistency, and I am able to do almost all that God can do. What therefore can you make of me but God.'

He is the husband of the church and as such wears a ring, indicating her perpetual betrothal to himself. Thousands upon thousands kneel before him, they struggle to get near his person: they stretch forth their hands to obtain his indulgences, and crave his divine benediction.

All power is delivered unto him. He forgives sins; he bestows grace; he cancels punishments, even in purgatory. He restores the lapsed; he excommunicates the rebellious; he can make that which is unlawful, lawful; he cannot err; his sentences are final; his utterances infallible; his decrees irreformable. Pope Boniface VIII stated:

> 'The Pope alone is called Most Holy, Divine Monarch, Supreme Emperor, King of Kings.'

Rome, the woman of the Apocalypse, surely is full of names of blasphemy. Pages could be written of her boastful, self-glorification and outrageous blasphemy, but enough has been said to get the point over; except to add, during the Protestant Reformation, Pope Julius issued a medal in 1550 which threatened Protestant Britain with destruction. The medal bore the words:

> 'The nation and Kingdom that will not serve thee (the Pope) will perish.'

The Daily Telegraph of March 11th 1988, carried a report of how Dr. Clifford Hill ripped his 'dog-collar' in half to represent God's anger against the Anglican Church. He called Anglicans in the congregation to stand and repent of unbelief in the Church, as well as its moral failings. Questions need to be asked! What about the Anglican Church's moves towards uniting with Rome? Is all the talk on the ordination of women, unbelief and moral failings, a smoke screen to cover up the real issue – **the reuniting of the Anglican Church with the Church of Rome?** Why do the present day prophets remain silent on this most vital and important issue? Leaders of the Anglican Church who work for unity with Rome are traitors to the Gospel of Jesus Christ by even considering moves towards reuniting with Rome. Why do the present day prophets not call the Anglican Church to repent of their involvement with Rome – the whore of the Apocalypse? Why do they remain silent with no words of rebuke or condemnation upon the Roman Catholic Church and its unbiblical heresies? After all is said and done, the Anglican Church does not, as yet, teach or believe in purgatory, penance, veneration of saints, Mary worship, veneration of the Pope, confession, indulgences, transubstantiation, Peter the rock, etc. etc. etc. If the one who is looked upon by the majority in Britain as the present day prophet be a true prophet of God, he needs to address the real issue – the moves of the Anglican Church to reunite with Rome!

Do we suppose that the Anglican Church has escaped the infiltrating effects of Rome's Jesuit priests? No, they have done all in their power to discredit the Protestant Church of England, in the sight of the people. What do you think of Archbishop Runcie's working group to examine the Law Commission's recommendations on blasphemy? Does it give the scent of Jesuit influence? It does not take much leaven in the Anglican (or any other) loaf to leaven the whole loaf.

Article from the Daily Telegraph, Thursday, 3 March, 1988, by R Barry O'Brien, headlined, Blasphemy Law should 'cover all religions'.

> 'A new law to make blasphemy an offence against all religions, and not just Christianity, has been urged by a Church of England working group.
>
> In a report to the Lord Chancellor, Lord Mackay of Clashfern, the group recommends that the existing common law offences of blasphemy and blasphemous libel should be abolished, and replaced by a new statutory offence, penalising insults to any faith.
>
> Blasphemy has been defined by judges as material that reviles, vilifies or insults God, Christ, the Bible or the beliefs and doctrines of Christian churches, but it

is not an offence under existing law to insult non-Christian beliefs or doctrines.

The Church of England group echoes the view of Lord Scarman in a blasphemy case in 1979 that the law should be extended to protect the religious beliefs and feelings of non-Christians.

In an increasingly plural society like modern Britain, it was necessary 'not only to protect them from scurrility, vilification, ridicule and contempt,' said Lord Scarman.

The group, chaired by the Bishop of London, Dr Leonard, disagrees with the majority recommendation by the Law Commission in 1985, that the existing offences of blasphemy should be abolished and not replaced.

'Freedom of religion is an internationally recognised human right. Feelings of reverence for the sacred should not be undermined, whether by explicit or implicits permissions of abusive attacks upon them,' says the group.

The group was set up in 1985 by the Archbishop of Canterbury, Dr Runcie, to examine the Law Commission's recommendations. The members included Prof Keith Ward, of London University, and the Bishop of St Albans, the Rt Rev John Taylor.

The Archbishop has sent its report to the Lord Chancellor with a letter endorsing the recommendation.'

The noose around the neck of those who contend for the faith tightens.

Whether we believe it or not, we are once again in the old battle, which we thought had been won at the Reformation. The battle is the struggle between the priests of Rome and the people of Britain. The days of the Reformation will soon, once again, be upon us. Rome has already gained a section of the Anglican clergy, who have adopted her principles, use her worship and teach her dogmas. She has members in the House of Commons, who think, speak and vote as she desires, through which she brings pressure to bear on Goverment policies. In Parliament, she is strong, and moves members through their constituences. She works incessantly through the press. She is served by a host of devoted troops, who work under all sorts of names, in all places and disguises, she has her reporters and writers for the press, preachers in the pulpits of Protestant denominations, masters of schools, inspectors and examiners. Even Prince Charles, the heir to the Protestant crown, has not escaped. He accepted an invitation to attend a Catholic Mass on 21st September, 1986, in Cumbria.

The headline in the Catholic Herald of 26.9.86 stated:

'Prince Stirs the Hearts of His Catholic Subjects.'

Fifty years ago there were less than five hundred Roman priests in Great Britain; today there are thousands. Fifty years ago there were no monastries at all in Great Britain; today there are over two hundred. Fifty years ago there were not five hundred chapels; today there are nearly two thousand.

It is for you to decide whether you will let her master you.

## The Woman Further Identified

*'And the woman was arrayed in purple and scarlet colours, and decked with gold and precious stones and pearls . . .'* (Rev 17:4)

The above scripture perfectly fits the description of a papal enthronement. When a newly elected Pope presents himself in public for the first time, he appears wearing five different articles of scarlet coloured clothing, a pearl covered vest, and his mitre is adorned with gold and precious stones. The heirarchy attending him in his great ceremony of enthronement are all dressed in purple.

*' . . . having a golden cup in her hand full of abominations and filthiness of her fornication'*. (Rev 17:4)

The Cup of Abominations.

Unwittingly fulfilling scripture, the Papacy took the symbol of the woman and the cup to be her very own emblem in 1825.

The cup full of abominations are her Satan-inspired doctrines, which stand in opposition to the Holy Scriptures, being full of filthy spiritual prostitution.

*'The seven heads are seven mountains, on which the woman sitteth.'* (Rev 17:9)

Rome has been known through the generations as the city of the seven hills.

*'And the woman which thou sawest, is that great city which reigneth (note 'reigneth' – 'still reigns') over the kings of the earth.'* (Rev 17:18)

The Popes of Rome certainly have fulfilled the claim of reigning over the kings of the earth. The following words were addressed to Pope Martin V:

'The most Holy and most blessed, who holds the celestial jurisdiction, who is Lord over all the earth, the successor of St Peter, the anointed, the ruler of the universe, the Father of Kings, the light of the world.'

Such words will not go unpunished by the one and only Holy Father of the everlasting Trinity.

*'And upon her forehead was a name written MYSTERY BABYLON THE GREAT, THE MOTHER OF HARLOTS AND ABOMINATIONS OF THE EARTH.'* (Rev 17:5)

The true character of Babylon's ancient occult religion was never concealed. 'Mystery' Babylon is so named because her true identity has been covered up. It is a 'mystery', and not what it seems; for it professes to be divine, but in character is satanic.

Until a short time ago I believed that the 'woman of the Apocalypse' and her 'scarlet coloured beast' were two separate evil powers, vieing for world dominion. I was deceived by the mystery of iniquity, through my involvement in ecumenical circles; if we touch tar a little sticks. After I renounced and repented of my involvement with ecumenism, I was able to see the true identity of the Beast.

Without any shadow of doubt, the woman seated on the scarlet coloured beast with the name Mystery Babylon written on her forehead is Rome, and all that the Papacy stands for. She is the mother of harlots and abominations of the earth, therefore in her is to be found the root of every false doctrine and occult practise of the earth.

Romanists themselves agree that Rome is signified in the Apocalypse by the name 'Babylon the Great', but argue that 'Babylon the Great' seated on the seven hills was the ancient Babylonian religion; the Rome of the Caesars and not the Rome of the Popes. As earlier mentioned, the character of Babylon's ancient religion was never concealed. The title, 'Mystery Babylon', shows her to be the Rome of the Popes; she is a 'mystery' religion, and not what she would have us all believe she is. Whilst professing to be divine, she is, in actual fact, totally Satan-inspired, and is guilty of the most abominable blasphemy against the Holy Trinity.

> *'And I saw the woman drunken with the blood of the saints, and with the blood of the martyrs of Jesus: and when I saw her, I wondered with great admiration.'*
>
> (Rev 17:6)

Our brief look into history has shown how Rome has been guilty of the murder of multitudes of

God's people. She has drunk the blood of the saints and martyrs of Jesus with such greediness, that she has intoxicated herself with it.

> ' . . . *and I will tell thee the mystery of the woman, and of the beast that carrieth her, which hath seven heads and ten horns.*' (Rev 17:7)

The seven heads have a double significance. Seven mountains – the seven hills on which Rome stands and seven kings – seven sorts of governments. Five of these were extinct in John's day, one was then in being, and the other was yet to come. (See Rev 17:9–10).

The ten horns are ten kings which have received no kingdom as yet, (in John's day) but receive power as kings one hour with the beast. (See Rev 17:12).

> '*The beast that thou sawest WAS, AND IS NOT; and shall ascend out of the bottomless pit, and go into perdition: and they that dwell on the earth shall wonder, whose names were not written in the book of life from the foundations of the world, when they behold the beast THAT WAS, AND IS NOT, AND YET IS.*' (Rev 17:8)

The rule of Rome has never, since it first commenced, ceased to exist, save once, for a very brief period during the Gothic invasions. It was a secular, pagan power for five to six centuries and has been an ecclesiastical paganised form of Christianity ever since. There lay a brief period between these two main stages when the great city received a blow from her Gothic captors.

So who is the beast?

There is the beast that WAS, then it WAS NOT, and yet, it still is!

The beast that was – Babylon's ancient occult religion and political power.

The beast that is not – Fall of Babylon's ancient occult religion and political power for a short time during the Gothic invasions which took place in 476 AD. The Beast that yet is – Revival of Babylon's ancient occult religion, which took on the form of 'paganised Christianity' in Constantine's day, and adopted the name of the Roman Catholic Church. The ten horns or kingdoms give the beast strength and represent the political side of the Papacy.

Pope Boniface VIII declared:

'There is one Holy Catholic Church . . . and we are instructed in the words of the gospel, that there are two swords, the spiritual and the temporal.

Each is in the power of the church, to wit, the spiritual sword and the material sword. But the latter is to be used for the church. The former by the hands of the priests, the latter by the hands of kings and soldiers, yet according to the permission of the priest. One sword must be under the other sword and the temporal authority must be subject to the spiritual power.'

Why was such a declaration necessary? It was all part of Anti-christ's plan to wipe out Protestantism.

Rome ruled the known world at the first advent of Jesus, and will once again rule the world just prior to the second coming of Jesus.

' . . . *and causeth the earth and them which dwell therein to worship the first beast, whose deadly wound was healed.*' (Rev 13:12)

The mystery of iniquity was already at work in Paul's day, and is responsible for the acceleration of the Apostasy over the past 1900 years. As no one man could have possible lived during the whole duration of apostasy it can be seen that Anti-christ is not an individual but is represented in the entire dynasty of Popes. The final reigning Pope of this dispensation will be revealed in the flesh as the 'man of sin', the son of perdition. He will be the false prophet and head of the Apostate world church.

He will not be an open opponent of Jesus Christ: Anti-christ means 'other Christ', 'substitute Christ', or as the Pope claims to be, Vicar of Christ. He is adored on earth as 'representative of Deity'.

By taking the title 'Holy Father', the Popes of Rome have robbed the Creator of the Universe, the One and Only Holy Father, of the worship and adoration that is due only to Him.

By taking the title 'Vicar of Christ', the Popes of Rome have robbed the blessed Holy Ghost of His position and ministry in the Church.

By praying to Mary, the Popes of Rome deny that Jesus Christ is the only mediator of the New Covenant.

*'They profess that they know God; but in works they deny him.'* (Titus 1:16)

## Come Out of Her, My People

*'And I heard another voice from heaven, saying, Come out of her, my people, that ye be not partakers of her sins,*

*and that ye receive not her plagues, for her sins have reached unto heaven, and God hath remembered her iniqities.'* (Rev 18:4–5)

God is here giving warning to all who belong to Him:

*'Come out of mystery Babylon, the Mother of Harlots and Abominations of the Earth'* (Revelation 17:5)

*'Have no fellowship with the unfruitful works of darkness, but rather reprove them'* (Ephesians 5:11)

*'Be ye not unequally yoked together with unbelievers: for what fellowship hath righteousness with unrighteousness? and what communion hath light with darkness?*

*And what concord hath Christ with Belial? or what part hath he that believeth with an infidel?*

*And what agreement hath the temple of God with idols? for ye are the temple of the living God; as God hath said, I will dwell in them, and walk in them; and I will be their God, and they shall be my people.*

*Wherefore come out from among them, and be ye separate, saith the Lord, and touch not the unclean thing; and I will receive you,*

*And will be a Father unto you, and ye shall be my sons and daughters, saith the Lord Almighty.'*

(2 Corinthians 6:14–18)

## The Destruction of Rome – The Woman of the Apocalypse

*'Therefore shall her plagues come in one day, death, and mourning, and famine; and she shall be utterly burned with fire: for strong is the Lord God who judgeth her.* (v8)

*And the kings of the earth, who have committed fornication and lived deliciously with her, shall bewail her, and lament for her, when they shall see the smoke of her burning.* (v9)

*Standing afar off for the fear of her torment, saying, Alas, alas that great city Babylon, that mighty city! for in one hour is thy judgment come.* (v10)

*'For in one hour so great riches is come to nought. And every shipmaster, and all the company in ships, and sailors, and as many as trade by sea, stood afar off,* (v17)

*And cried when they saw the smoke of her burning, saying, What city is like unto this great city!* (v18)

*And they cast dust on their heads, and cried, weeping and wailing, saying, Alas, alas that great city, wherein were made rich all that had ships in the sea by reason of her costliness! for in one hour is she made desolate.* (v19)

*Rejoice over her, thou heaven, and ye holy apostles and prophets; for God hath avenged you on her.* (v20)

*And a mighty angel took up a stone like a great millstone, and cast it into the sea, saying, Thus with violence shall that great city Babylon be thrown down, and shall be found no more at all.* (v21)

*And the voice of the harpers, and musicians, and of pipers, and trumpeters, shall be heard no more at all in thee; and no craftsman, of whatsoever craft he be, shall be found any more in thee; and the sound of a millstone shall be heard no more at all in thee;* (v22)

*And the light of a candle shall shine no more at all in thee; and the voice of the bridegroom and of the bride shall be heard no more at all in thee: for thy merchants were the great men of the earth; for by thy sorceries were all nations deceived.* (v23)

*And in her was found the blood of prophets, and of saints, and of all that were slain upon the earth.* (v24)

(Revelation chapter 18)

The destruction of the great whore is total devastation. There has been no promise or provision made in the Word of God to restore Papal Rome, only judgment, ruin and annihilation. God will avenge the blood of the faithful, who 'protested' against the heresies of Romanism. He will reward her doubly for all the wars and revolutions which she has incited and inspired, for in her was found the blood of the prophets and of saints, and of all that were slain upon the earth.

## The Last Call

Hear the word of the Lord. Come out of her, my people! Come out of her, my people! All who refuse to hear the Word of the Lord will become intoxicated with the wine of the whore's fornication. The conscience of disobedient, rebellious children will be seared as with a hot iron.

John Knox, the Scottish Reformer stated: 'the Pope is the head of the Kirk of Antichrist . . . the Roman Catholic Church is the synagogue of Satan, and the head thereof called the Pope, the man of sin of whom the Apostle speaketh'.

Bishop Ridley, the English Reformer who was burned at the stake, declared: 'The seat of Rome is the seat of Satan . . . and the Bishop thereof is the Antichrist himself indeed.'

Thomas Cranmer, the first Protestant Archbishop of Canterbury, said: 'As for the Pope I refuse him, as Christ's enemy and Antichrist with all his false doctrines.'

John Wycliffe, Martin Luther, John Calvin, William Tyndale, and John Wesley, branded the whole succession of Popes as Antichrist.

When Bible-believing Christians look into the doctrines and practises of the Roman Catholic Church, they can come to no other conclusion, and have to agree, that the Church of Rome is indeed the Apostate Church – the Church of Antichrist – the synagogue of Satan.

True believers need to face up to the fact that the present-day Pope has a global policy of 'Peace and Unity', through which he aims to win the inhabitants of the earth into his fold of deceit and deception.

In the days which lie ahead, prior to the second coming of our Lord, the religious deception will intensify, true believers will be hated, persecuted and killed because of their love for the Lord, and the truth of His Word. We can face all that lies ahead with all confidence, knowing that 'His grace will be sufficient for us'.

*Brethren, 'Let us who are of the day, be sober, putting on the breastplate of faith and love, and for an helmet, the hope of salvation.*

*For God hath not appointed us to wrath, but to obtain salvation by our Lord Jesus Christ.*

*Who died for us, that whether we wake or sleep, we should live together with him.*

*Wherefore comfort yourselves together, and edify one another, even as also ye do.*

*Now we exhort you brethren, warn them that are unruly, comfort the feebleminded, support the weak, be patient towards all men.*

*See that none render evil for evil unto any man; but ever follow that which is good, both among yourselves and to all men.*

*Rejoice evermore.*

*Pray without ceasing,*

*In everything give thanks;*

*For this is the will of God in Christ Jesus concerning you.*

*Quench not the spirit:*

*Despise not prophesyings,*

*Prove all things; hold fast that which is good*

*Abstain from all appearance of evil.*

*And the very God of peace sanctify you wholly; and I pray God your whole spirit and soul and body be preserved blameless unto the coming of our Lord Jesus Christ.*

*Faithful is he that called you, who also will do it.'*

(1 Thess 5:8–24)

Alleluia! Alleluia! Alleluia! Alleluia! will be the cry of all true saints of the Most High when God finally judges Mystery Babylon. As seen in chapter nineteen of the book of Revelation, the saints will be in heaven, preparing for the wedding feast of the Lamb. Alleluia!

*'And after these things I heard a great voice of much people in heaven, saying, Alleluia; Salvation, and glory, and honour, and power, unto the Lord our God:* (v1)

*For true and righteous are his judgments: for he hath judged the great whore, which did corrupt the earth with her fornication, and hath avenged the blood of his servants at her hand.* (v2)

*And again they said, Alleluia. And her smoke rose up for ever and ever.* (v3)

*Let us be glad and rejoice, and give honour to him: for the marriage of the Lamb is come, and his wife hath made herself ready.* (v7)

*And to her was granted that she should be arrayed in fine linen, clean and white: for the fine linen is the righteousness of saints.* (v8) (Revelation chapter 19.)

Will you hear the Word of the Lord and what the Holy Spirit is saying to the Bride? Let the final words not be mine but those of Him with whom we have to do:

***'Come out of Her, My People!'***

# Audio Tapes and Books

## General

**A1 TESTIMONY I**
Includes Isabel's conversion and her initial visit to the Philippine Islands.

**A2 TESTIMONY II**
Includes Isabel's second visit to the Philippine Islands.

**A3 THE POWER OF THE TONGUE**
Faith in God, or positive confession?

**A5 GOD'S PLAN OF SALVATION**
Excellent tape to bring family and friends to Jesus!

**A13 OUR HEAVENLY LANGUAGE**
The Baptism of the Holy Spirit, the reasons for, and the importance of, praying in tongues.

**A24 TESTIMONY III**
Isabel's Travels in 1987

**A26 YOU MUST BE BORN AGAIN**

**A27 AS IT WAS IN THE DAYS OF NOAH**

**A28 THE ORIGIN OF SATAN**

## Healing

**A4 THE EVERLASTING COVENANT**
The full significance of the Lord's Supper explained.

**A6 OBEDIENCE TO THE WORD**
Accepting the Word of God and acting upon it.

**A7 HIS GRACE IS SUFFICIENT**
Stand on God's Word and defy the enemy.

**A8 THOU SHALT HAVE NO OTHER GODS**
For the Lord, He is a jealous God.

**A16 DOES GOD HEAL EVERYONE?**
Reasons why some are healed and others are not.

**A19 HAVING DONE ALL – STAND!**
By His stripes you were healed.

## End Time Prophecy

**A9 DAYS OF PREPARATION**
Preparation for the Lord's return.

**A10 THE MARK OF THE BEAST**
The 'End Times' with special reference to the impending 'cashless society.'

**A11 THE SEVEN TRUMPETS**
The 'End Times' with special reference to the exodus of the Jews from Russia.

**A12 THE GLORY OF THE LATTER HOUSE**
Does this refer to the 'Church' or to the Children of Israel?

**A14 A CHOSEN PEOPLE**
Preparation of the Bride of Christ.

**A15 COME OUT OF HER, MY PEOPLE**
Comparing the Doctrine of Rome with the Word of God.

**A18 BE NOT DECEIVED**
Beware the New Age Movement

**A20 BEWARE ECUMENISM!**
Do not be deceived by words of 'peace, love and unity'.

**A21 REVIVAL OR PERSECUTION?**
Should we believe in visions of mere men, or the Word of God?

**A22 THE TEN VIRGINS**
The 'foolish virgins' will not enter the Kingdom of Heaven.

**A23 WE MUST MAKE A STAND**
We must not compromise with heretical doctrines.

**A25 THE GREAT FALLING AWAY**
Are you discerning the 'apostasy' of our day?

## Music

**M3 Praise and Worship**
**M4 Piano Praise**

## Books

**Arise and Reap**
**Reaping with Joy**
**Come out of Her, My People**

**I.C.M. (A/V Dept.)**
PO Box 10, Ulverston, Cumbria LA12 8HR
**AUDIO TAPE & BOOK ORDER FORM**

Please complete this form and send it to the above address together with the cost. Cheques payable to I.C.M. (A/V) please.

AUDIOTAPE ....................................................................................
(Name and number of tape)

NAME AND ADDRESS ....................................................................
(Block letters please)

....................................................................................

**PRICES:**

| | | |
|---|---|---|
| AUDIOTAPES | £3.00 (+ 35p p&p) | |
| REAPING WITH JOY | £2.95 (+ 40p p&p) | I enclose a cheque for .................. |
| ARISE AND REAP | £1.95 (+ 40p p&p) | |
| COME OUT OF HER, MY PEOPLE | £2.50 (+ 40p p&p) | Signed .................................... |
| COMPLETE SET OF AUDIO TAPES | £75 (+ £3 p&p) (27 Teaching and 2 Music) | |

Our prayer is that you will be blessed by, and that God will be glorified in and through these tapes.

# Video

## General

**V.I. TESTIMONY**
Testimony and explanation of the 'fall of man.' Satan's defeat and man's restoration.

**V.2. TESTIMONY III.**
Isabel's travels in 1987

**V.3. THE POWER OF THE TONGUE**
Faith in God or 'positive confession?'

**V.T.3. OUR COMFORTER – THE HOLY SPIRIT**
The Baptism of the Holy Spirit, the reasons for, and importance of, praying in tongues.

## Healing

**V.4. THE EVERLASTING COVENANT**
The full significance of the Lord's Supper explained.

**V.5. DOES GOD HEAL EVERYONE?**
Some reasons why some are healed and others not.

**V.6. OBEDIENCE TO THE WORD.**
Accepting the word of God and acting upon it.

**V.8. THOU SHALT HAVE NO OTHER GODS**
For the Lord, He is a jealous God.

## End Time Prophecy

**V.T.6. A CHOSEN PEOPLE**
Preparation of the Bride of Christ.

**V.11. THE SEVEN TRUMPETS**
The 'End Times' with special reference to the exodus of the Jews from Russia.

**V.13. DAYS OF PREPARATION**
Preparation for the Lord's return.

**V.15. COME OUT OF HER, MY PEOPLE!**
Comparing the Doctrine of Rome with the Word of God.

**V.21. REVIVAL OR PERSECUTION?**
Should we believe in visions of mere man, or God's Word?

**V.22. THE TEN VIRGINS**
The 'foolish virgins' will not enter the Kindgom of Heaven.

## Philippine Films

**P.1, 2 & 3. CHILDREN AND TEENAGERS OF THE PHILIPPINES.**
Three films in one of the lifestyle of the Filipinos and the work of the Holy Spirit amongst them.

**P.4. MINISTRY IN LEWAN**
Journey to Lewan and the work of the Holy Spirit in a jungle area.

**P.5. SUMADEL**
Life and ministry in a primitive village high in the mountains.

**P.6. VISIT TO A LEPER COLONY**
Miracles amongst the lepers, and the abominations that bring disease and poverty upon a nation.
(Parents! – please view before showing children)

All profits from the sale of these tapes go back into the work of proclaiming the Gospel of Jesus Christ.

The quality of the indoor sequences in the Philippine films is of inferior quality compared to the British ones, due to poor local conditions.

e.g. – no electricity – All power was produced by a generator and batteries.

**For optimum picture quality, it may be necessary to adjust the tracking control on your video recorder. Adjustment of your TV may also be needed.**

Thank you for your support.
*With love in Jesus' service.*
**Isabel Chapman**

Purchase price of each tape £15 & £1 p&p. Total £16

Tapes may be hired for £5 per tape per week and £1 p&p. Total £6

If you wish to purchase a tape having seen it, please send a further £10 within the due date.

**I.C.M. (A/V Dept.)**

PO Box 10, Ulverston, Cumbria LA12 8HR

**VIDEO-TAPE ORDER AND HIRE FORM**

Please state:

| Tape No. | Title | Buy | Hire | VHS/Beta |
|---|---|---|---|---|
| | | | | |
| | | | | |
| | | | | |
| | | | | |

NAME AND ADDRESS ..............................................................................
(BLOCK CAPITALS PLEASE)

..............................................................................TEL. NO..........................

I enclose cheque/PO for ........................................ Signed ........................................
Cheques payable to I.C.M. (A/V) please.

Our prayer is that you will be blessed by, and that God will be glorified in and through these tapes.